SOME

ADJUSTMENT

REQUIRED

?

TIM SWEETMAN

Scripture references are from the following bible translations:

GNT

KJV

ERV

NIV

Amplified

Foreword

The title of this book ends with a question mark, asking the reader to formulate his or her own opinion about the subjects covered by Tim. It is a helpful question mark as it makes us realise that we take too much for granted without questioning the validity of what we do and think.

"Some adjustment required?" exposes some of the traditions and misunderstandings we have accepted for too long in our Christian experience and gives us permission to change; permission to be different.

This book is written for a generation wanting reality. It cuts into the unreality which brings spiritual death and releases the reader into a closer appreciation of the life which God offers us today.

John Sweetman

Author

Acknowledgements

In the putting together of this book I would like to thank John, my brother, for the tireless corrections of grammar and doctrine and also for the very many suggested re wordings.

I would also like to thank my family for their encouraging words and patience.

The completion of a book is never the work of one person alone but a combination of many contributors both locally and also down through the years of learning to adjust and rethink.

I am grateful to Father who has nudged and taught and revealed so much to me over many a long period.

I pray that you too learn to be nudged and taught and are able to adjust accordingly.

Some Adjustment Required?

A book to raise more questions than answers perhaps!

Jesus said, "You will know the truth, and the truth will set you free" *John 8. 32.*

Conversely, if we don't know the truth then we will most certainly remain in slavery and not be free.

The enemy will always attempt to spread confusion and dismay.

"Arm yourself with truth so that you are able to overcome the enemy." *Ephesians. 6: 10 – 18.*

....

Preface

"Some adjustment required?" started life some fifty years ago, during 1968, after a dream I had in which I saw a preacher teaching from the pulpit.

In my dream the preacher's head slowly changed to take on the appearance of a wolf's head.

It was then that I heard very clearly the Lord saying in my dream, "my people are being taught lies in my name".

From that time I have reassessed my understanding and studied God's word more thoroughly. My understanding of what I thought I knew well has changed dramatically and my mind has been realigned accordingly.

This book is partly a result of that continuing change of understanding of God's Kingdom and is written with the aim of giving us, the readers; the opportunity to reassess our understanding of what life is about. What is God's Kingdom? Where do we fit in and why are we here?

What is our purpose in God's Kingdom?

Chapters

The Bible

Within this book there are many references to a book called the Bible.

The Bible is the # 1 bestselling book in the world.

It is in many ways an instruction manual that is written in order to show us the best way to live the life that God has given us.

The Bible is a book that gives us a proper perspective on God's dealings with us, mankind.

It also gives us an insight into God's master plan for His creation from the beginning of all things until on into eternity.

The Bible is a love letter written by the creator to us His creation.

Once saved, always saved?

Let's begin our search by making sure that we are standing on solid ground shall we?

What does the term 'being saved' really mean anyway?

Many go to church week after week believing that by doing so there is a guaranteed place reserved in heaven for us when we finally breathe our last breath.

On the face of it, we all appear to be fine people.

We are quite nice to each other, we don't swear or drink excessively, and we have good jobs and are responsible people for the most part.

On the outside we seem to be very nice people indeed.

But do we know Jesus?

For that matter, does anyone know Jesus?

Now that's a strange question you might think.

'I wonder why that matters'?

You might even ask, 'how does anyone know Jesus'?

Is it really possible to know Jesus?

You see this question goes right to the basic question about our own place in eternity and reflects how far we have come from understanding why Jesus came to earth to die at all.

In fact it also reflects how much we misunderstand about the Kingdom that Jesus preached about.

In the book of Matthew 7: 21-23 we can read about a conversation that Jesus had while he was on earth.

He was talking to the many people who had come to hear him teach.

I have written here what Jesus says to them.

"Not everyone who calls me Lord will enter God's kingdom. The only people who will enter are those who do what my Father in heaven wants. On that last Day many will call me Lord. They will say, 'Lord, Lord, by the power of your name we spoke for God. And by your name we forced out demons and did many miracles.' Then I will tell those people clearly, 'Get away from me, you people who do wrong. I never knew you.'

Can you hear those words of Jesus echoing? *'I never knew you'.*

Jesus isn't referring to the people around him or to those who lived in his time on earth; he is referring to people who have lived since his resurrection.

That includes you and me.

The only criterion that Jesus places on people entering God's Kingdom is what?

To know Jesus.

Really? What about all the charity workers? What about all those peace keepers? What about all of those.........

Jesus says that the only ones who get to enter God's Kingdom are those who know Him.

Amazingly Jesus even talks about people who have done many miracles! - People who have spoken out about God; people who preached on the streets perhaps or organised Evangelistic Crusades.

What really? Even those sorts of people might not know Jesus? Is that really what Jesus said?

You know it is so very easy to get wrapped up and carried along with the gifts that God gives us.

One man might be given a gift of healing for example. He may well use that gift to heal many thousands of people. He may even raise the dead.

Another man may have a gift of evangelism and apparently bring many into God's Kingdom and yet not know Jesus; not hear that small quiet voice of command.

It is possible to do all of that and yet to be too wrapped up in the flow of the events to hear God's quiet voice.

God will not take back his gift. Once given, that gift remains in the possession of the receiver. The gift may well take control unless the receiver spends time listening, getting to know the voice of the giver.

What a sad situation, when at the end of that career the receiver hears those words, *'I never knew you'.*

It is very possible for a person to commit themselves to following Jesus initially but then to run with the flow of whatever is happening. Perhaps in a very charismatic church for example, to just follow the crowd, go to the groups, sing the songs, say the words but not really spend any time with Jesus.

Problems come along and with the help of friends we get through them.

But did we spend time with Jesus? Did we find out what he was telling us through it all?

Was our character strengthened? Did we get closer to Jesus through it?

Or was it just a blip in life and after it was over we struggled on?

Many people within church congregations also experience this life style.

Folk turn up at the door week after week. They listen to the sermons, sing the songs, chat to the person sitting next to them and then go home again, never experiencing Jesus.

Our time with Jesus is so crucial. It is during those times that our relationship with him is established and strengthened.

We may have many friends and strong relationships. We may have many gifts and great personality. We may do many good and noble things, be a great ambassador in the church we go to but if we don't know Jesus then all of that is just dead works and will all be burnt up as being useless.

And so we can see that knowing Jesus is not only possible but also incredibly necessary.

At the end of the conversation that Jesus had recorded in Matthew 7: 21 -23 we hear him saying that not only does he not know the people concerned, but he actually calls them 'people who do wrong'.

The amplified version of the Bible explains that Jesus is calling them *'people who act wickedly'* (disregarding his commands).

Remember now we are discussing people who on the face of it have spent their lives working miracles and speaking on behalf of God, casting out demons in Jesus' name.

Jesus describes these as people who act wickedly because they disregard his Father's commands.

They didn't listen to hear his voice. They didn't know him.

Acting under our own steam and ignoring Father's command is just the same as acting in rebellion to God.

If we are acting in self will then we are acting in opposition to God, regardless of the works that are carried out.

If we return to the conversation that Jesus was having with the crowd as recorded in Matthew 7: 21 -23 we find that one of the criteria for knowing Jesus is *'to do what Father in heaven wants' vs 21.*

Obedience

In order to be obedient it is vital to be able to hear the command.

How can we hear the command if we don't listen if we don't spend time in his company learning how to hear his voice?

We can be as active as we like, but at the end of the day activity isn't what we are called for.

We are called in order to be in relationship with Jesus.

We need to listen in order to be effective and useful in God's Kingdom.

Knowing Jesus is imperative.

It goes without saying that knowing the person who gave his life so that we could be redeemed would normally be an automatic course of events but surprisingly many people are deceived into leaving that relationship unfulfilled.

Can you imagine that anyone would want to run away from having a close relationship with the God of love?

It happens.

I will let you in on a secret shall I?

In the same way that children learn to have good relationships with their natural parents by being obedient and learning to trust the parent's judgement so it is the same with our own relationship with Jesus.

From trust flows love and friendship.

Obedience – knowing Jesus

We have discovered that one of the main criteria for gaining access to and staying in God's Kingdom is obedience.

Clearly, in the illustration in the last chapter we saw how it is possible to enter God's Kingdom and to also receive spiritual gifts and yet not be aware that we have moved away from him.

We need to be aware that moving away from Jesus or worse, not knowing him in the first place is the same as not living in God's Kingdom.

Keeping a close relationship with Jesus is vital in order to remain inside of God's Kingdom.

Learning to hear his voice and to be obedient is key here.

It is odd therefore that entry to his Kingdom is where many fall short, even at the first hurdle.

In John chapter 3, we read about a man called Nicodemus who came to Jesus secretly in order to ask about how to gain entry and Jesus explained to him that he must be born again.

Nicodemus didn't understand and so Jesus went on to explain that in order to be re-born into God's family it is necessary to be baptised in water and that once baptised in water the Spirit of God will take root and then he will become a new creation.

Baptism in water is the first step into God's Kingdom.

It is a step of faith for us.

Faith is the stuff that brings things into being.

As we step into the waters of baptism, believing that Jesus died in order for us to live then we certainly come up out of the waters a new creation - a Spirit filled creation. Born newly into God's family - born of God himself.

In the book of Acts 2:38 Peter talks about the same thing.

'Peter said to them, "Change your hearts and lives and be baptized, each one of you, in the name of Jesus Christ. Then God will forgive your sins, and you will receive the gift of the Holy Spirit'.

We can see then that baptism is the very first step on our part - a step of faith and an act of obedience in God's Kingdom and yet so many refuse to take that step.

I hear so many 'buts'.

'But', I was christened at birth, I don't need baptism!

'But' I would look silly in the water!

'But' can't I just believe in God without being baptised? My friend does!

'But 'if God loved me he wouldn't want me to do that!

'But' I'm allergic to water!

'But' it's an old fashioned idea!

'But' I'm too old!

'But' surely I can get in without being baptised? They don't do that at 'my church'!

Jesus often used to refer to the difference between sheep and goats.

At one time he said, 'my sheep hear my voice'.

My sheep listen to my voice. I know them, and they follow me. I give my sheep eternal life. They will never die, and no one can take them out of my hand.

John 10:27-28 ERV

Sheep follow Jesus.

Goats on the other hand are full of 'buts'.

Sheep don't ask 'why'? Sheep don't ask 'what if', sheep don't complain or object.

Sheep simply hear the shepherd's voice and follow knowing that the shepherd cares about them and will find the best places for them to eat.

The shepherd knows the best way for the sheep.

Obedient sheep get to "lie down in green pastures".

We will find that life in God's Kingdom goes better when we have learnt to be obedient.

Our God is a great shepherd. He knows how to look after His sheep.

The Creation

Genesis Ch. 1 and 2.

In the first book of the Bible - the book of Genesis, we read an account of the creation of the universe.

Within this account we also read about the first people that relate to God.

There is some discussion around this theme as to whether God created the universe in seven literal days or whether, as scientists suggest, it took somewhat longer for man to come to maturity.

I do not intend to propose that I have a complete and definitive answer to this discussion but I am able to perhaps offer a few suggestions in order to assist with a better understanding.

It is worth noting that the book of Genesis was never intended to be a scientific archive.

The book of Genesis is a book of beginnings - hence its name Genesis.

The beginning

The account of the creation was first handed down by word of mouth from generation to generation.

Each family and tribe and each early nation will have had the account of the creation retold time and time again over many centuries until it was eventually written down by scribes probably during the time of the prophet Samuel at the time of the early Israelite settlements in the promised land.

The accuracy of the account of God's early dealings with man cannot really be questioned in the light of the fact that each family for generations will have memorised and recounted the facts over and over again so many innumerable times.

When family tribes gathered together the accounts again would have been shared and verified.

No doubt mighty men of God such as Enoch and Methuselah, Noah and others would have discussed the origin of things with God also.

There aren't too many generations between the death of Adam and Noah when detailed accounts began to be written down.

The account of the Genesis and what actually happened during the early period of man and how and why the separation from God, the creator, occurred must have been so devastating - so monumental an event that no detail would be forgotten or changed within the families of the descendants of the followers of God.

I think that we can assume that the prehistoric references with regards to the separation of the waters, and the appearance of land, the placing of the stars in the sky and the sun and the moon in their place to be for signs and indications, for special meetings and occurrences must have come directly from God himself and drawn from conversation with the first man and woman as they walked in perfect unity all of those years ago. How many years or centuries that the first man and woman walked and talked with God in the garden that was prepared for them we are not told.

We can imagine the excitement as God recounted to Adam the arrival of fishes and birds and other animals and then the arrival of man, in the same way that a parent might recount the arrival of a new baby child to a toddler.

"and then you came along"!

Of course we cannot know how those conversations went exactly or how much early man and woman understood. What they realised is that God was all in all. The creator of all things.

They understood that God has an order and a purpose in all that he did and does.

They recalled that one event followed another and that God set his seal of approval upon it.

They understood that God spoke all of creation into existence.

What the dynamics of that creation was they needn't have understood in detail. It wasn't important.

They understood God's order in creation. There were stages, or periods of creation. Certain things happened during specific periods or times. They discovered that those times can be divided into six distinct periods. Periods of time can also be translated as days.

In fact, elsewhere in Genesis the same word translated as *'day'* is translated as *'age'*.

Scientists today can confirm that the account of Genesis in terms of the order of how things came about is factually correct. That's not really a surprise for some of us.

In the bible God often uses numbers to describe various things.

The number three for example illustrates strength.

The number seven illustrates completeness.

In the book of Genesis the creation is described as being brought about in six 'days'. 'God saw that it was very good, and on the seventh day, God rested'.

Seven is the number of completeness.

When God had finished, creation was 'complete'. There was nothing more to do.

In the book of Genesis chapter one, from the very beginning of all things and throughout the process, we read eight times throughout the creation period, the phrase, *"and then God said"*.

For me it brings to mind the picture of a patient creator just waiting and waiting for that period to come to the perfect time for the next period to start. *"and then God said"*.

So, we've got vegetation on the go and it's working well, we are ready for the next stage, *"and then God said"*.

Each stage was commenced with a word from the creator.

Can we imagine the enthusiasm as God retold the events to the first man and woman and how the excitement would also have continued as the story was retold down through the generations?

Please don't misunderstand what I am saying here.

I have no doubt at all that God could easily have created the whole of the universe in six literal days. He could have created it in an instant. With God anything is possible.

I am simply giving here an alternative thought. A different understanding of what the book of Genesis is actually telling us.

For God to nurture creation over a period of billions of years, carefully, lovingly nudging it all into perfection for me indicates what a loving faithful and caring God he is.

How greatly he loves us, knowing what the future held and yet how much he wanted us to be a part of him.

We now come to the very awkward appearance of Adam and Eve.

I have no problem with the fact that science apparently disagrees with the exact facts as we perceive them to be recounted in Genesis but do we understand the book of Genesis correctly?

Again, I have no doubt that God is more than able to create man out of the dust of the earth and to also in turn, create woman from one of his ribs.

However, why don't we rethink or read again this account to see if the writer is describing another different series of events.

How does a child explain his or her own birth?

It is interesting that the wording with regards to the creation of Adam is very similar to the wording in the New Testament as Jesus breathes life into his disciples.

When Jesus breathes new life into the disciples the disciples are changed, through the gift of the Spirit, as we are when born again, into a new creation.

Because of what Jesus has done, his victory on the cross, we are become a new man; a new creation.

This doesn't mean however that before our new birth our bodies did not exist, very clearly they did. And yet we are a new creation as Adam and Eve, the first man and woman, were.

Genesis talks about God making man out of the dust of the earth and scientists do agree that man originated in the dust of the earth.

I was not there and cannot therefore give an eye witness account of events but given the above scenario as we see, or imagine God patiently watching over as all of creation develops, nurturing and speaking direction into each situation, let us also imagine the emergence of man as a thinking individual, rising up from the ground to eventually walk on two legs.

Can we then imagine a period when finally man has an awareness of a creator?

Perhaps there comes a point in creation when man is aware of and can communicate and relate with God?

Perhaps after all those billions of years as God patiently waits and nurtures his creation there comes a realisation amongst his created that there is something else outside of man?

We can then read Genesis differently and see that God did create 'Adam' from the dust of the earth, in his origin.

The word *Adam* or *Adama*, means *'dust of the earth, with red (blood).*

We can perhaps imagine how then prehistoric man developed to a point of recognition of God and then "God breathed life into him". God's Spirit entered man.

In the same or in a similar manner that Jesus breathed new life into the disciples gathered together after his resurrection.

A new creation had begun. Man now had relationship with God.

God did indeed create man from the dust of the earth and God also breathed 'life' into him as the book of Genesis relates.

So, what about Eve, the first woman?

I am not a scientist or a genealogist; I don't profess to understand scientifically how the two sexes became separate.

The Bible explains that God took a rib from Adam and created the woman from that rib.

Something was taken from man in order to create two different biological species.

I am OK with that personally but maybe we could expand the narrative a little?

There is an awful lot that God wants us to know about marital relationships and much can be understood from that illustration in Genesis but perhaps that will be a lesson for another time.

Here I am entering very deep muddy and previously unknown waters so be patient.

Apparently, animal biologists explain, and I believe them, two different sexual species occurred some 2.5 billion years ago.

These species are called Eukaryotic and were the first creatures that required two opposite sexes in order to mate and reproduce.

God had nudged creation in order to produce two different sexes.

I don't pretend to understand why God arranged for it to be necessary for there to be two sexes in order for us to mate and reproduce but that appears to be the way that he has designed it.

There is a lot that we can discuss here with regards to there only being two different sexes but let's move on.

We can imagine therefore the scene in Genesis chapter two as God introduces Adam to the animals that have been created and asks Adam to prophesy over them, to give them their names and characters.

We can imagine too, God giving Adam authority to care for the animals, birds and plants and shows him that these aren't suitable partners for him - that Adam needs a helper - someone to complement him in every way.

God, the creator, then breathes Spirit life into the woman, Eve that he, so long ago, divided from the man.

We might also imagine over a period of time, how God teaches Adam the nature of the relationship between a man and a woman.

I am sure that God revealed to Adam and Eve much of what we don't understand today in our own relationships together.

The man and woman became one. They understood their purpose and their place in the universe in communion with God.

God walked and talked with both Adam, the first man and Eve, the first woman in the garden that he had created for them to live in.

Now, please don't misunderstand me here. I have stated before that I have no doubt that the narrative within the Genesis story could have occurred exactly as laid out as we have historically read and understood it in the first few chapters.

God is amazing and can do amazing things, in an instant.

Here I am simply allowing us to obtain a deeper understanding of Gods nature and character.

The book of Genesis was never intended to be a scientific or historical outline of what we now call pre-history.

The book is about God's purpose in creation and his relationship with man.

I am sure that there are many alternative scenarios that we might imagine within the Genesis narrative.

What we need to remember and to be clear about is that God cannot lie. His word is true for all time.

However, our understanding and current revelation of his word is sometimes and perhaps often, cloudy and unclear.

We must always read and teach his word with some humility, preferring to live in unity with those of a differing viewpoint rather than squabble over things which, ultimately may be of little importance.

What we know is that God the creator brought all things into existence with a word.

That God brought order and perfection out of nothing.

That God's primary purpose in all of creation is to have relationship - unity with man.

On that note I would like to ask you, the reader a question or two that perhaps you might like to think about.

Q. If the universe that God created was good and complete, why was it necessary to then create a 'garden' for Adam and Eve to live in?

Q. What was the nature of that 'garden'?

A garden is often referred to in the bible as a place of rest and sanctuary.

God's Kingdom - How do I get in?

At the beginning of chapter one, we asked the question, what does the term 'being saved' mean any way?

In my last book, 'Journey into Life', I gave readers a picture of travelling to a foreign country in order to gain entry to God's Kingdom.

God's Kingdom is very much a real place that we can enter immediately if we choose to do so.

Many people know about heaven, that it is a place where God lives. It is his dwelling place.

We have been taught that if we believe in Jesus and are baptised then we can go to heaven when we die.

This fact is true but misses the point completely.

In fact God's Kingdom is a place that we are invited to live in now whilst we are alive on earth.

God's Kingdom is the place that existed before we drew away from God.

It is the place that we can return to.

Jesus and his disciples all taught about God's Kingdom.

The whole purpose that Jesus came to earth was to teach about the Kingdom of God and to defeat the enemy that had caused a rift between us and God.

He did that completely and entirely when he offered himself as a pure sinless human as a sacrifice in order to buy back the entire human race, which includes you and I.

Allow me to try to explain further.

Just imagine for a moment that there was nothing that separated us from God. Imagine that we could just simply walk straight into His Kingdom - into His very presence.

Think seriously about that.

What do you think there is that exists at the moment that separates us from God?

Why do you think that we can't just talk naturally to God?

The reason is, as you probably realise, is that God is Holy and we are not.

The reason for that is that we do things we shouldn't. I won't give you a list but you know what I am talking about here.

That situation hasn't always been the case.

When we were first created, as discussed in the last chapter, we had access to God and chatted to Him naturally all the time. We lived in His presence.

Imagine that!

Then something happened that separated us from God.

We, that is, God's created beings, were deceitful - we sinned, in other words we rebelled against God.

We can read about our time with God and the events of the rebellion in Genesis 2:7 – 3:25.

It's true that our rebellion was motivated by the enemy, satan who wanted to see us fall down because he hates us, but the responsibility was ours, or *Adam's*, the first man.

Because of that original rebellion against God, all of creation has lived under the curse of death - separation from God, who is life itself.

That is why we can't just go in and chat to him now in the same way as the first man and woman did. Sin has created an obstacle - a wide chasm that nothing can bridge.

Or at least that used to be the case until Jesus came!

As you know, Jesus came to earth teaching about the Kingdom of God and he said that The Kingdom of God is at hand. That means it is within our grasp - At our fingertips!

Jesus came in order to overturn the curse of death.

The fact is that, because Jesus, the perfect sinless man, gave his own life as a sacrifice in order to pay the price of death for us, we can now walk into God's Kingdom - into Gods presence, today!

The way is clear. There is no longer any chasm or separation from God for us if we choose to trust that Jesus death and resurrection paid the price for us.

Jesus is called 'the redeemer' because he redeemed us. That means that he paid for us.

Clearly we could never do anything of ourselves that would be good enough to get us back to God. All we ever do is get things wrong and make matters worse.

Even if we worked all our lives carrying out charitable acts and gave away all of our money and belongings, that wouldn't be enough to bridge the gap between us and God. Our sinful nature would still be there!

But Jesus paid for us, even if we don't deserve it. And we really don't, do we? Be honest.

But amazingly God loved us so much that he sent Jesus to die in order to redeem us - John 3:16.

So we are free to walk into God's Kingdom at will if we believe or trust that Jesus' death is sufficient to redeem us.

Jesus was once asked by a man called Nicodemus, what he had to do to be saved? Jesus' answer was that he had to be born again!

That was a strange answer wasn't it. You could read about it in John 3.

Jesus went on to explain that when we realise and admit that we are in fact sinful and can't get back to God on our own merit and apologise to God for the way that we live, we can begin to understand that what Jesus achieved on our behalf is the only way that we are able to change.

When we realise how we are and what Jesus has done for us we can be baptised in water and God's Spirit will take root in us. We then become a new creation - born again a new person - born straight into God's Kingdom - into God's own family.

This is what is meant when we talk about 'being saved'.

We are saved from our old life which will inevitably lead to eternal death and brought straight into a new relationship with God - into an abundant and eternal life.

Saved indeed!

When we are born again into God's family we can start learning how to live in the way that we were created to - in relationship with God.

Once we have come into his Kingdom the Spirit who is sown in us takes root and our thought patterns and our behaviour begin to change as our mind is renewed.

This change is described in the Bible by a Greek word - 'metanoia'.

Metanoia means to have our minds retuned to be in line with God's mind.

We will come across this 'Metanoia' again later but I have written about this in my previous book called 'Journey into Life'. Take a look.

God's Kingdom is for us and for now.

So, it is probably a good time to sit down and think about how saved are we?

- Have we realised that we need God because of our bad character?
- Have we apologised and asked Him to save us?
- Have we been baptised in water in order to come into His family?
- Have we been restored by the Spirit of God?
- Do we have that relationship with God?

Discipleship.

The term 'disciple', seems to be almost holy in its description doesn't it?

In fact, a disciple is simply a person who is learning from someone else.

In the ancient world of Israel, a travelling rabbi (a rabbi is another name for teacher), might have had several pupils who would follow him around and they would learn as they go. The pupils would be called 'disciples'.

Jesus was a rabbi and therefore the people who followed him and learnt from him were called his disciples.

Some disciples are specifically mentioned by name in the Bible. These disciples faithfully taught what they had heard from Jesus.

The people who were taught by those disciples were also called disciples of Jesus as they learnt the things that Jesus taught.

A disciple is a person; man or woman, who is learning a new discipline. The words are similar.

All Christians are expected to be disciples; as we are learning a new way of living from an excellent teacher - the Spirit of God.

If we are learning how to live differently; being taught by the Spirit, then we are disciples. We are learning a new discipline.

In much the same way as you might go to a fitness club in order to learn how to become fit, we are learning how to become like Christ.

That is where the word 'Christian' comes from; we are learning to become 'Christ like'. Or 'Christ-ones'.

It is a discipline that we are following; therefore we too are disciples.

We have now come into discipleship.

Discipleship for a Christian living in God's Kingdom is a way of life.

There is a very deceptive teaching amongst some that declares that if a person 'commits their life' to Jesus then there is no more that needs to be done.

The claim is that from that point on, the person is somehow 'protected' through life regardless of the life they lead, and that they will, one day be mystically transported to heaven.

From what we have read in Matthew 7: 21 -23 in our first chapter: 'once saved always saved?", we know that this teaching cannot be true.

There is no 'quick fix' to heaven.

Whilst it is true that there is nothing that we can do of ourselves that can enable us to live in God's Kingdom (it is all as a result of what Jesus has already achieved), how we respond to God matters very much.

Our personal walk with God, in his Kingdom, during this life will determine our place, if any, with him in eternity.

Would you like to just read that paragraph again?

Our personal walk with God, which is our relationship with Jesus, in his Kingdom, during this life, will determine our place, if any, with him in eternity.

But, you say, I thought it was just a question of taking Jesus into my heart and then I get to go to heaven one day?

Sadly that is what is being taught to many.

The truth is that Jesus cares about our relationship with Him and came to earth in order to tell people that 'The Kingdom of God is at hand'.

When Jesus died and rose again in victory three days later The Kingdom of God on earth became fact.

Walking into and living in God's Kingdom or not, is a decision for us to make now while we are here on earth.

Leaving God's Kingdom also is a decision that we make when we don't take the time to establish that relationship with Jesus.

Did you really believe that God sent his only son, Jesus, into the world to die so that we could sign on the dotted line and then ignore him?

God loved the world so much that he sent Jesus in order to have a relationship with us.

With God it's always been about relationship.

Relationship is what holds The Kingdom in place.

'My sheep', said Jesus, *'they hear my voice'*.

Learning to hear the voice of Jesus is an ongoing lesson.

Relationships are not built instantly; they take time to build and to mature.

This is why we need to stay close to Jesus - to devote time in learning his ways and his teachings.

As we spend time with him then we too change to be like him.

Our thoughts will change, our character changes, our motivation changes.

This is what discipleship is - learning to be like the teacher.

God is Love.

This is the essence of God.

Love is what he is made of.

Can you imagine how we might change as the very essence of God starts to manifest itself in us as well?

Can you imagine a body of people dripping with the essence of God?

If that excites you then keep on being a disciple.

Saints:

The title 'saint' is also a misunderstanding.

It is because we are disciples that we too are 'saints'.

The word saint comes from the Latin, *'Sanctus'*.

Sanctus means holy.

The Catholic Church and to a lesser degree, the Church of England, make much of 'saints'; giving them a hierarchy and power that they do not have.

You and I are saints - every Christian that ever lived is a saint.

The word saint was widely used in letters in the Bible where the writers address a local group of Christians.

They might write to 'the saints at Corinth', or to 'the saints at Ephesus'.

Paul for example writes in his letter to the Ephesians, "to the saints who are in Ephesus".

The writers are writing to those Christians who were living in God's kingdom; referring to them as 'holy people'.

We too are holy people; we are separated from the world and brought into a holy union with God.

We are saints if we are living within God's Kingdom.

There is no hierarchy of *'saints'*.

It is not possible to pray to particular saints, for example, as, firstly, they won't hear us and, secondly, to do so would be to act in rebellion towards God.

God has told us not to attempt to speak to the dead. The named saints that religious organisations propose that we pray to are all dead to the world.

He has also said that we should not have any other gods but Him - however minor.

This would include Jesus' mother - Mary and would also include any other person who has died, regardless of how well regarded they may have been.

When a Christian dies their reward is in heaven. They cease to relate to earth or to the people that remain on earth in any way.

You and I are saints. All Christians, both alive and dead can be referred to as saints - We are all holy people - set aside and joined to a Holy God.

Angels

I have heard many people talk about their deceased friends and relatives as being 'angels' in heaven.

This is clearly a misunderstanding.

Humans do not turn into angels at the point of death.

Angels are a separate type of creation to humans.

Angels are God's messengers and have many purposes.

They were created in order to carry out certain functions and to do God's bidding.

There are thousands upon thousands of angels.

They all differ in appearance and purpose.

There are different jobs to do within the angelic realm.

There are archangels, seraphim and cherubim to name just three types.

Michael, Gabriel and Lucifer are three angels that are mentioned in the Bible.

According to the Bible, Michael and Gabriel appear to be arch angels who look after and organise thousands upon thousands of other angels, as Lucifer may have been before he was ejected from God's presence.

There are angels that are created in order to war against the enemy and others that guard certain areas in God's kingdom.

There are angels that sing praises continuously around the throne room of God. There are also mighty angels that are responsible for whole nations. There are angels that are responsible for you and I and angels who go to and from the heavens performing God's will.

Angels have always desired to look into God's dealings with man. They are curious. They have a different relationship to God than ours.

Angels are often called upon to deliver messages from God and to minister to people on earth.

When they appear in the world they often seem to be radiant with light. I guess that's what happens when you spend time with God!

When God gave the Law to Moses, it was given through the angels.

There is considerable agreement through the bible that God used the angels as intermediaries when He gave the Law to Moses even though the text in Exodus and Deuteronomy implies that He gave it directly.

In fact the Greek version of Deut 33:2 states that the Lord came to Sinai with myriads of His angels. Acts 7:53 and Hebrews 2:2 also confirm the angels were the intermediaries of the Law.

When Jesus was in the desert, after he had been baptised, having fasted for forty days and nights, many angels came to minister to him. Matt 4:11

When the enemy rebelled against God and was thrown out of God's heaven, a third of heaven's angels rebelled with him and were also thrown out.

The enemy and the rebellious angels that were thrown out of heaven are now forced to remain on earth and yet Satan appears to be allowed to come into God's presence in his position as a representative as we can read about in the book of Job.

These demonic beings have taken many unwitting individuals captive and also have influence over whole areas and nations. One of our purposes and the reason that Jesus came to earth is to bring freedom to the world (people), from the slavery that these demonic beings have inflicted– in order to give us victory over these fallen angels, also called demons.

It is these creatures; now severely disfigured, distorted and marred, that continuously war against God's Kingdom and to that end, seek our demise.

It is interesting to note that Satan is able to appear as an angel of 'light' in order to deceive us.

And no wonder, for even Satan disguises himself as an angel of light.

2 Corinthians 11:14 ESV

The enemy's deception often appears to be helpful initially.

We are very vulnerable whilst grieving for a loved one for example, or during some traumatic event.

This can often be a time of deception for many.

It is at times like this when our defences are low that the enemy whispers lies into our ears - confusions and misconceptions, half truths told about those around us perhaps leading to mistrust of breakdown of relationship.

It is not until we are enslaved in mistrust or even worse that the truth becomes clear, often too late.

Perhaps the development of an addiction might begin with a desire for comfort. At first the initial pleasure brings relief but very soon the pleasure creates it's own need and becomes a habit.

This is why we must always be on our guard against deception.

Jesus referred to these fallen angels as "unclean spirits", and "demons".

Jesus dismissed them with a word.

Christians also have been given authority over these demonic beings in order to bring freedom to others and to restore all that the enemy has destroyed.

We are forbidden to worship angels of any description.

It is worth noting that there are twice as many angels that are loyal to God as there are fallen angels.

What is God's Kingdom?

In my last book, 'Journey into Life', I talked about the reason that Jesus came to earth. What did he teach about?

Jesus' whole life was dedicated to ushering in God's Kingdom.

He taught that it was 'at hand', meaning that it was within our grasp.

Jesus taught that God's Kingdom was about to be presented to people on the earth.

When Jesus died on the cross, He exclaimed 'it is finished'. His mission and victory was complete.

The way had been established for anyone to walk into God's Kingdom.

So let's see if we can find out what God's Kingdom actually looks like shall we?

Jesus gave many examples of what God's Kingdom is like.

He used parables, that is stories, in order to describe it but the people that he talked to didn't really understand what he was talking about at the time.

I am always discovering new things hidden within Jesus' parables- I'm sure that you will too.

When we talk about a kingdom we are normally describing an area belonging to a person or a group of people with a certain way of life and who follow certain rules governing the land.

God's Kingdom is an expression of God's character.

In order to find out what life in God's Kingdom is like, we need to look into God's character.

God is love

That is an odd expression, isn't it? And a difficult concept to grasp.

The reality is that God doesn't just love. He Himself is love.

How can God be made of love?

We think of love as being a fuzzy emotion that sometimes affects our thinking.

But Love has many aspects to it.

Paul wrote about some aspects of love in his letter to the Corinthians.

Love endures with patience and serenity,

Love is kind and thoughtful, and is not jealous or envious;

Love does not brag and is not proud or arrogant.

It is not rude; it is not self-seeking, it is not provoked [nor overly sensitive and easily angered]; it does not take into account a wrong endured.

It does not rejoice at injustice, but rejoices with the truth [when right and truth prevail].

Love bears all things [regardless of what comes],

believes all things [looking for the best in each one],

hopes all things [remaining steadfast during difficult times],

endures all things [without weakening].

Love never fails.

1 CORINTHIANS 13:4-7 AMP

Love is not a fuzzy emotion but an active agent.

Love is active and responsive in what it does and also in what it doesn't do.

We need to take each of those aspects of love that Paul was writing about and look at how they might be exhibited in life in order to see and experience how love is expressed.

If we were able to squeeze God like an orange then what would flow out would be love.

In fact we can actually see what love looks like when we look at Jesus' life. In all that he said and did, love flowed out of him.

Life in God's Kingdom is an expression of God's love lived in an ever increasing reality of that love being expressed in life.

Learning to live in the character of love is an activity which will affect the whole of our lives in all aspects of living.

We only learn how to live that type of love by keeping close to God and listening to him as Spirit talks to us.

Whilst love is a natural fruit of the Spirit and will occur in our lives as naturally as apples do on an apple tree, the closer that we are to God then the more productive that love will be.

In the same way that a fruit tree, when watered and nourished and pruned and fed, produces good fruit - free from bugs and diseases, so will we if we spend time in the presence of Spirit.

Love is active and tangible.

God is Spirit

When we think of God our minds often refer back to pictures that we have seen in art galleries or in books of God sitting in the clouds. These pictures are a deception of the facts really.

We forget that God is Spirit.

God is invisible and yet his reality is tangible.

Jesus came to earth as flesh and blood as we are, but God is Spirit.

The Kingdom of God, therefore, is also a Spirit filled Kingdom.

That too is an odd concept isn't it.

So, how do we as flesh and blood creatures live in a Spirit fuelled Kingdom that is built on this fluid active thing called love?

To begin with, entry into God's Kingdom comes about as a result of our realisation that we are sinners. We have done wrong things, yes, but more than that, our way of life and our thoughts are lived outside of God. We need God in order to bring us back into a relationship with him.

This is the start of our journey and some people call it repentance. Really it is a desire for a change of mind - a change of the way we think and live.

The bible uses a Greek word to describe it - *Metanoia*. It means having our minds changed to think the way that God thinks.

The prophet Isaiah talks about the difference between our thoughts and God's thoughts:

The Lord says, "My thoughts are not like yours. Your ways are not like mine. Just as the heavens are higher than the earth, so my ways are higher than your ways, and my thoughts are higher than your thoughts.

Isaiah 55:8-9 ERV

Because of the way we have lived - the things we have been taught and the things we have done and experienced, the things that we read and watch on TV, our broken relationships and deceitful ways - our minds have become corrupted and we have lost the ability to see things clearly in the way that God does.

Without God's intervention there is no way that we are able to get our minds and actions corrected.

When God's Spirit enters our life then our minds can be renewed - changed for good.

This is what that Greek word, *Metanoia* refers to.

Jesus said that once we realise that we need to change then we also need to be baptised in water.

Baptism in water is our entry into God's Kingdom. Through baptism in water we are born into God's family, we become sons and daughters of God Himself.

God places his seal on our life by baptising us in His own Spirit

Jesus' sacrifice and resurrection enabled this to happen.

We come into God's Kingdom by believing in and trusting in Jesus and, having made that decision, through baptism in water.

In baptism, Spirit, the Spirit who is God, becomes one with us.

Yes, you read that correctly.

The Spirit, who is God, becomes one with us when we come into God's Kingdom.

We are not just God's children in some metaphysical sense but we are actually God's children - one with God.

This is a fact that is not widely realised or appreciated, which is why so many Christians apparently hop between the two kingdoms with ease.

We become one with God through His Spirit when we leave behind the old Kingdom of death and move into God's Kingdom of life.

If Christians understood this reality then they would also realise why it is therefore impossible to join in union with someone who is not 'one' with God.

Paul wrote about this in a letter to his friends at Corinth.

You are not the same as those who don't believe. So don't join yourselves to them. Good and evil don't belong together. Light and darkness cannot share the same room.

2 Corinthians 6:14 ERV

How can we and also God be so joined to someone who is not living in his Kingdom?

This goes for any type of union, whether financial or emotional. How can we as Christians being one with God, make a contract with someone outside of God? Can we unite God with the world in that way? When we look at it like that we clearly cannot.

But let's return to God's Kingdom.

God is Spirit. We have become Spirit people - a new creation - born from God.

When we first come into God's Kingdom, we initially continue in the old ways that we thought and acted.

As we allow God's Spirit to teach us we learn to become Spirit people. Our minds are renewed and our actions and responses change.

God's Kingdom is filled with people - all at varying stages of learning and changing.

As we learn to live in love then God's Spirit produces 'fruit' from that love in different forms.

Paul wrote about the fruit that comes from the Spirit in a letter that he wrote to the Galatians.

The fruit that the Spirit produces in a person's life is love, joy, peace, patience, kindness, goodness, faithfulness, gentleness, and self-control.

Galatians 5:22-23 ERV

Take a look for yourself.

These are all characteristics that just come naturally in time to all who live close to God in His Kingdom.

Training

Whilst living in God's Kingdom is a pleasure and also a privilege, full of life and change, it is also a place of training - we are being trained.

What are we being trained for?

In short, the answer to that question is that we are being trained to overcome the enemy who is Satan.

We have left the enemy's kingdom now and we are living in God's Kingdom.

As we learn to take on more of God's character of love the enemy will become frustrated and upset and attempt to pull us back into his realm again.

We will learn how to overcome those attempts to disrupt us and to pull us down.

Satan always tries to hold us back and to undermine us, in many ways - we live in a war zone.

This too is a part of living in God's Kingdom. We learn to become overcomers.

Some Bible translations refer to overcomers as ones who have the victory or to those who are triumphant but the meaning is the same.

We might have a problem with fear for example or perhaps we are gossipers or maybe we have a problem with telling lies or an addiction, relationship issues, there are all sorts of things that can be a problem for us.

God wants us to learn to overcome these issues in our lives and also to help others to do the same. We can do that as we listen to Spirit and also unite with other Christians.

As we learn to overcome in those areas that God points out to us we also learn to love as He is love. God's character becomes our own.

As well as enabling us to grow and become mature people in God's Kingdom there are trophies and rewards for those who overcome the enemy.

It is clearly good for us to remain free and not tangled with problems which the enemy would love to get us tied up with but there are also additional advantages in overcoming him.

We will learn about this as we go along.

There are seven clear promises that are given to overcomers in the bible.

We can read about them in the book of revelation:

Rev 2:7 – 3:21 is about the rewards that are for those who are overcomers.

It appears from reading Rev. 2:26 that overcomers are the ones who will be reigning with Jesus for one thousand years and that they will be given responsibility over those who are being reigned over.

The responsibility that is given to them is dependent upon what they have achieved in this life with Spirit.

When Jesus comes again there will be a wedding feast, Jesus will claim his Bride - Jesus' bride are all those who have been made righteous by the blood of Jesus and have been overcomers in this life.

There will be others at the wedding feast.

As in all weddings there are friends of both the bride and the groom.

There are also those who make preparation for the ceremonies - the best man and there are guests at the wedding.

We will look at the rewards that are given to overcomers later and also who the other people at the wedding might be.

Who will get to reign with Jesus for one thousand years? That appears to be a responsibility that is strictly for the bride alone. We shall find out later.

Overcoming is all about working with God. There isn't anything that we can do on our own even with massive knowledge and determination. We will only ever be able to overcome by working with God - by hearing what he is saying in each situation and by being obedient.

Sometimes an occasion might require us to say one thing and on another occasion perhaps to say something else or to say nothing at all or to respond in a different way. We won't know unless we learn to listen.

That is how our relationship and closeness to him will grow.

If we do not overcome the issues that are in our lives or are unable to overcome; there is some compensation - eternal life yes, but how we will wish that we had waged war and won through whilst we had the opportunity here on earth in this life.

How we will wish that we had stretched our faith and trust.

How will we respond when asked about our life?

What a waste! This life is so short.

So, to recap, God's Kingdom is about :

- Living in love and allowing that love to change us.
- Living in faith - learning how to hear God and being obedient as we move forward.
- Learning to live dependant upon Spirit - allowing God to reign and rule in our thoughts and actions.
- Becoming trained in spiritual warfare - learning how to overcome in partnership with Spirit.
- Living in God's Kingdom is about losing our life and submitting to God's life rising up within us.
- It is about becoming one with God Himself.

As I discussed in 'Journey into Life', God's Kingdom is all about relationships - with each other and with God.

It is a swirling mix of change and realignment; of revelation and clarification.

Everything is new!

What is Faith?

We talked a little about faith earlier, but what exactly is faith?

We will find that faith plays a big part of living in God's Kingdom.

In a letter that was written to the Hebrews we find that:

Without faith no one can please God. Whoever comes to God must believe that he is real and that he rewards those who sincerely try to find him.

Hebrews 11:6 ERV

Without faith it is impossible to please God.

We need to have faith in whatever we do, otherwise we are not pleasing God.

It is a big issue if we want to please God then, isn't it?

Of course we want to please God in what we do and say. It appears that we need to have this thing called faith in order to do that.

I will try to explain.

When we speak we say what we believe is true.

What we say is what we have faith in - it is what we believe.

Truth only comes from God but often what we believe is a result of the way that we lived before we came into God's Kingdom - it is often confused and incorrect.

For example we might have some strange ideas in our heads that are not correct. If we carry on living according to those incorrect ideas then we won't be pleasing God, we will be pleasing ourselves.

It is necessary to hear what God is saying in order to allow our minds to be retuned. Do you remember when we discussed that Greek word - 'metanoia'?

In that way we are able to think God thoughts and in turn to speak God's words. Accordingly our actions and motivations will also be God's. This will affect the way that we live, which in turn will bear good things and the things that we think, say and do will become noticeable also to others around - they will see how God has changed our lives.

This is how faith brings things into being that formerly did not exist.

Faith changes things.

Apart from pleasing God, which is why we are here, we also need to have faith in order to defeat the enemy.

We talked a little about being overcomers earlier.

It seems that we need faith in order to do that too.

We will find that it's an essential piece of our armour enabling us to advance and to take down those strongholds that stand against us – against God.

Faith also is our protection against further attack.

If you think that this sounds a bit like a war zone then you would be correct, that's exactly what it is.

We are living in a spiritual war zone. The enemy wants to pull us down and destroy us. We are a threat to his rule.

We need to realise this and to equip ourselves accordingly.

So what is faith?

In the book of Hebrews we find that *Faith is what makes real the things we hope for. It is proof of what we cannot see.*

Hebrews 11:1 ERV

Having faith brings things into reality that weren't there before.

Faith can be a positive thing but it can also be a negative thing.

If we continually believe that bad things are going to happen in our lives then they surely will.

Our thoughts and words and actions will bring about the bad things that we experience.

That is the result of negative faith.

On the other hand, if we listen to what God the Spirit is saying to us by reading and by hearing his promises to us we begin to believe and consequently talk about the good things that he promises us. We start to live in His promises and His goodness becomes a fact in our life.

That too is faith bringing about things that weren't there before.

So faith is first planted in our thoughts. Then through our thoughts into our words and actions, bringing about what God has planted there.

We can see then that faith isn't something that we can muster up ourselves. Faith comes from thoughts that God the Spirit places within us.

We need to listen to Spirit in order to hear those God thoughts.

It is often easier to listen to what the enemy says to us and to believe that.

The enemy has many ways to plant incorrect thoughts and ideas into our mind.

Bad news, unpleasant experience, broken relationships, television programmes, unpleasant reading material and both Christian and non Christian friends can all feed us thoughts that don't come from God. We do need to safeguard what we allow to enter our head as that in turn affects the way that we think.

So what sort of things will stretch our faith in order to help us to grow?

Paul wrote to his Roman friends about this.

So then faith comes by hearing, and hearing by the word of God.

Romans 10:17

Faith grows by the word of God.

The word of God is what God the Spirit whispers to us and can also be things that we read in the Bible.

We will find all sorts of promises about our future and the way God thinks about us in the Bible.

Finding out what he thinks about us and who we now are might be surprising and will also encourage us to find out more.

When we read or hear and understand who we are and what our purpose is then our faith will grow because we will realise that God has great plans for us.

Trust what he says. That is another way of describing faith. Faith is believing what God says.

When our own situation or circumstances appear to be not what God says then that is the time to use our faith. Our circumstances cannot oppose what God says.

As we believe God, trusting in what he says, then our circumstances must change.

'Faith comes by hearing God'.

Faith only comes by hearing God for our self.

If someone has told you that fairies are real, then no amount of faith will make it so.

Believing in fairies may bring about a change in our mind but it will not be good. It will create delusional thinking and confusion.

That is what will happen by believing lies or deceit.

Many people hear from a preacher that they will be healed and go home believing it to be so only to find that they are not healed at all but have been deceived.

Faith in a preacher will not produce faith that is positive leading to growth.

God may use preachers or others in order to bring healing or some other thing into our lives but we need to hear from God correctly if that is the case.

We need to believe truth and that truth only comes from God.

Faith is built on having an intimate relationship with Him.

That relationship will not be built by trusting in another regardless of how charismatic they may be.

God wants to build our faith by having that personal relationship with Him alone.

He will train us and build us in order to make our faith strong so that when our faith is tested it will not fail.

We first have faith when we come into God's Kingdom.

That is our first step of faith. We trust in the saving redemptive power of Jesus in order to save us.

We trust that all of our sins are forgiven and destroyed for good.

We trust that God sees us through the sacrifice of Jesus as holy and sinless.

These are all steps of faith that we might not realise that we have taken.

Trusting in God will always place us on a firm footing.

Trusting in people or events sometimes makes us feel uneasy and concerned doesn't it?

When we place our trust, our faith in what God says then we can be sure that He will not fail to bring about what He has promised.

When we come into God's Kingdom then we begin to learn that we can place our trust in Him entirely.

We don't need to be concerned about our welfare, our income, our health, our relationships or any other thing if we place our faith in God because as we learn to hand those things over to Him we find that He is always faithful with what we trust Him with.

We live, in God's Kingdom, by believing and not by seeing.

2 Cor. 5:7.

Income

Let's look at just one aspect of our faith in God. We can then apply the same principles to every area of our lives.

One day when Jesus was out walking with his followers he realised that they were concerned about money.

They had left their regular paid jobs and steady incomes to be His disciples and now they didn't know where their money would be coming from.

Jesus said these things to them.

"So I tell you, don't worry about the things you need to live—what you will eat, drink, or wear.

Life is more important than food, and the body is more important than what you put on it.

Look at the birds. They don't plant, harvest, or save food in barns, but your heavenly Father feeds them.

Don't you know you are worth much more than they are? You cannot add any time to your life by worrying about it. "And why do you worry about clothes? Look at the wildflowers in the field. See how they grow. They don't work or make clothes for themselves.

But I tell you that even Solomon, the great and rich king, was not dressed as beautifully as one of these flowers. If God makes what grows in the field so beautiful, what do you think he will do for you? It's just grass—one day it's alive, and the next day someone throws it into a fire. But God cares enough to make it beautiful. Surely he will do much more for you.

Your faith is so small! "Don't worry and say, 'What will we eat?' or 'What will we drink?' or 'What will we wear?' That's what those people who don't know God are always thinking about.

Don't worry, because your Father in heaven knows that you need all these things.

What you should want most is God's kingdom and doing what he wants you to do. Then he will give you all these other things you need.

So don't worry about tomorrow. Each day has enough trouble of its own. Tomorrow will have its own worries.

Matthew 6:25-34 ERV

When we put God first in our lives, in everything that we do, then we don't need to be concerned about our own welfare as God will always provide what we need for that time.

Where do we place our trust (faith)?

Many people are dependent upon their employer in order to have sufficient income to live. If we are not employed, in the west we are dependent upon the state to supply our needs.

If we live in a country where there is no state support we might look to our friends or relatives to support us.

We place our trust (faith) in our employer or in the state or on others to provide for us.

It is good to work. It is good for us and good for others.

It is also good to share what we have with those who perhaps don't have enough.

However, we shouldn't be dependent upon either our ability to work or on our employer or the state or others to provide for us.

If we do so then we are looking to those places to meet our needs. We are replacing God by those sources.

We need to learn to rethink where we place our trust. Is it in those other sources or are we wholly dependent upon God?

If we learn to reassess where our dependency lies then we might find that by mentally placing God as our source of supply reaps enormous benefits in terms of placing our relationship with God in a correct perspective.

If we continue to treat the other sources as our dependency of supply then we are in effect treating them as God. They have become a replacement for where God wants our dependency to be.

We need to learn to rely on God completely in all things and not put anything or anyone in His place.

If we do that then we certainly won't worry when any particular source of income dries up. We will be living in an ever flowing stream of financial security that will never dry up.

This is another step of faith. Can we trust Him to supply all of our needs?

When we apply this principle of placing God at the centre of our lives and learn to become dependant upon only Him for all of our needs, whether that is financial, emotional, and spiritual or whatever that we need for life then we will find that we are standing upon a solid rock; a firm foundation that will never fail us.

Attack and defend

By faith we pull down the enemy and also we create a shield that will protect us from any attack.

Attack and overcome.

Faith is our weapon of attack.

Faith and dependency on God go hand in hand.

There have been many victorious battles won by simple faith in God.

I will list some of them here for you. I am sure that you will have heard of many but perhaps not realised that faith played the major role in the success.

My favourite battle that was won by faith is the battle of Jericho where the walls were brought down.

The following comes from the letter to the Hebrews, chapter 11.

It is a long section but well worth reading.

Faith is what makes real the things we hope for. It is proof of what we cannot see.

God was pleased with the people who lived a long time ago because they had faith like this.

Faith helps us understand that God created the whole world by his command. This means that the things we see were made by something that cannot be seen.

Cain and Abel both offered sacrifices to God. But Abel offered a better sacrifice to God because he had faith.

God said he was pleased with what Abel offered. And so God called him a good man because he had faith. Abel died, but through his faith he is still speaking.

Enoch was carried away from this earth, so he never died. The Scriptures tell us that before he was carried off, he was a man who pleased God. Later, no one knew where he was, because God had taken Enoch to be with him. This all happened because he had faith.

Without faith no one can please God. Whoever comes to God must believe that he is real and that he rewards those who sincerely try to find him.

Noah was warned by God about things that he could not yet see. But he had faith and respect for God, so he built a large boat to save his family. With his faith, Noah showed that the world was wrong. And he became one of those who are made right with God through faith.

God called Abraham to travel to another place that he promised to give him. Abraham did not know where that other place was. But he obeyed God and started traveling because he had faith. Abraham lived in the country that God promised to give him. He lived there like a visitor who did not belong. He did this because he had faith.

He lived in tents with Isaac and Jacob, who also received the same promise from God. Abraham was waiting for the city that has real foundations. He was waiting for the city that is planned and built by God.

Sarah was not able to have children, and Abraham was too old. But he had faith in God, trusting him to do what he promised. And so God made them able to have children. Abraham was so old he was almost dead. But from that one man came as many descendants as there are stars in the sky.

So many people came from him that they are like grains of sand on the seashore.

All these great people continued living with faith until they died. They did not get the things God promised his people. But they were happy just to see those promises coming far in the future.

They accepted the fact that they were like visitors and strangers here on earth. When people accept something like that, they show they are waiting for a country that will be their own. If they were thinking about the country they had left, they could have gone back. But they were waiting for a better country—a heavenly country.

So God is not ashamed to be called their God. And he has prepared a city for them.

God tested Abraham's faith. God told him to offer Isaac as a sacrifice. Abraham obeyed because he had faith. He already had the promises from God. And God had already said to him, "It is through Isaac that your descendants will come." But Abraham was ready to offer his only son. He did this because he had faith. He believed that God could raise people from death. And really, when God stopped Abraham from killing Isaac, it was as if he got him back from death.

Isaac blessed the future of Jacob and Esau. He did that because he had faith.

And Jacob, also because he had faith, blessed each one of Joseph's sons. He did this while he was dying, leaning on his rod and worshiping God.

And when Joseph was almost dead, he spoke about the people of Israel leaving Egypt. And he told them what they should do with his body. He did this because he had faith.

And the mother and father of Moses hid him for three months after he was born. They did this because they had faith. They saw that Moses was a beautiful baby. And they were not afraid to disobey the king's order.

Moses grew up and became a man. He refused to be called the son of Pharaoh's daughter. He chose not to enjoy the pleasures of sin that last such a short time. Instead, he chose to suffer with God's people. He did this because he had faith.

He thought it was better to suffer for the Messiah than to have all the treasures of Egypt. He was waiting for the reward that God would give him. Moses left Egypt because he had faith. He was not afraid of the king's anger. He continued strong as if he could see the God no one can see.

Moses prepared the Passover and spread the blood on the doorways of the people of Israel, so that the angel of death would not kill their firstborn sons. Moses did this because he had faith. And God's people all walked through the Red Sea as if it were dry land. They were able to do this because they had faith. But when the Egyptians tried to follow them, they were drowned.

And the walls of Jericho fell because of the faith of God's people. They marched around the walls for seven days, and then the walls fell.

And Rahab, the prostitute, welcomed the Israelite spies like friends. And because of her faith, she was not killed with the ones who refused to obey.

Do I need to give you more examples? I don't have enough time to tell you about Gideon, Barak, Samson, Jephthah, David, Samuel, and the prophets.

All of them had great faith. And with that faith they defeated kingdoms.

They did what was right, and God helped them in the ways he promised.

With their faith some people closed the mouths of lions. And some were able to stop blazing fires.

Others escaped from being killed with swords. Some who were weak were made strong. They became powerful in battle and defeated other armies.

Hebrews 11:34 ERV

We too can use our faith to win battles.

We might have been fighting battles for many years. That war can be won by hearing what God says about each battle and by acting on what he says. God's word mixed with our faith is a winning combination.

King David was a major player in living a life of faith in God and seeing God turn things around for him as a result of that faith.

He began his life of faith by starting small. He learnt to trust God when he was a young boy looking after his dad's sheep.

Once when a bear attacked he dared to defend the sheep by himself and God enabled him to win. The same thing happened when a lion attacked the sheep. David killed the lion as well.

So it was, when the huge and mighty Goliath attacked the Israelites everyone, including the king was afraid but David realised that because he had faith in God he would be able to overcome Goliath as well. God was faithful on every occasion.

In our own lives we learn faith by trusting God in the small things first.

As we find that he is faithful then our faith grows until we too bring down the Goliath's in our life.

A shield

And also use the shield of faith with which you can stop all the burning arrows that come from the Evil One.

Ephesians 6:16 ERV

In the above verse we find equipment that we can use very effectively in order to defend ourselves.

It is part of the armour that Paul listed in chapter six of his letter to the Ephesians.

The other items were all familiar to Paul and his readers at that time as they talk about the things that a Roman soldier might use in the course of his day. They illustrate the theme of attacking the enemy and being able to overcome. Take a look at what he is writing in his letter to the Ephesians ch. 6

The shield of faith is what we will look at here though.

Paul is saying that by using our faith as a shield we will be able to stop all of the burning arrows that come from the enemy.

What are burning arrows?

In Paul's time burning arrows would be fired from a bow in order to set fire to the surroundings and so cause havoc for a roman soldier.

The enemy sends burning arrows into our lives when he whispers untrue and deceitful thoughts in our head.

Thoughts that create mistrust of others, thoughts of our inadequacy, thoughts of envy, thoughts that God doesn't really care about us, thoughts that we don't have enough and thoughts that bad things are going to happen to us.

There are many such thoughts that the enemy attempts to plant in our mind causing pain and insecurity.

Our minds can be a minefield of doubt and fear unless we know God's truth and allow that to become a way of life for us.

God will retrain our mind with the truth, bringing security.

Faith is our shield against those fiery burning arrows.

Faith will ensure that those burning arrows can be quenched before they cause any harm.

Faith is a rock that we can depend upon.

In order to have faith we need to know in advance of those arrows being fired, where we stand and who we are in Christ.

We must be prepared in advance with knowledge of God's truth so that we can defend ourselves with the true facts as God has shown us.

Faith is our shield. Lies, fears and worries cannot take root in us as long as our shield is used.

The Roman small shield was a very crucial part of their armour and they knew how to use it effectively.

If we are to defend ourselves and overcome the enemy then we need to know how to use our faith effectively too.

because everyone who is a child of God has the power to win against the world. It is our faith that has won the victory against the world. So who wins against the world? Only those who believe that Jesus is the Son of God.

1 John 5:4-5 ERV.

Church

Well what can we say about this very mixed up and highly emotive subject?

In order to place ourselves on a good footing we had better begin with what Jesus said about it.

We find that the first mention of *'church'* in our Bible is in Matthew 16.18.

Jesus is talking to the disciples and in particular to Peter and He is saying:

So I tell you, you are Peter. And I will build my church on this rock. The power of death will not be able to defeat my church.

Matthew 16:18 ERV

We will put to one side what Jesus was referring to as *'this rock'* for now and come back to that later. It is a very important section of scripture.

For now let's look at what Jesus was talking about when he referred to *'my church'*.

In order to make sense of this we must first go back to the original Greek text that the verse was written in.

We might be very surprised at what we find.

The original Greek word - the word that Jesus used was *'Ekklesia'*.

Remember that word because we shall return to it.

When the Bible was translated into the English language the translators decided that instead of using a direct translation from *'Ekklesia'* they decided to use a different word instead.

The translators used the Greek word *'Kuriakos'*, which means in English, *'a possession of the lord'*. It is the same idea as in the old Scottish language a Kirk or Cirke would have belonged to the laird or lord in the area as would all of the property livestock and people.

So *'Kuriakos'* means belonging to a lord in the same way.

It is from this false substituted word *'Kuriakos'* that we get our English word church.

It is easy to see why the translators at the time might have looked around them to see all of the church buildings where the religious systems held their congregations and assumed that to change the word would suit their purposes and perhaps enable the congregations and priests to read it easier?

They used the word *'Kyriakos'* because *'church'* is all that they knew about.

But this is not what Jesus said.

'Kyriakos' is a word that neither Jesus nor His followers ever used.

Now the disciples when writing the gospels could have used the word *'Kuriakos'* but they purposefully didn't.

They used the word *'Ekklesia'*, as Jesus did, which means 'a people who are elected or called out'. It refers to a group of people who are called out for a specific purpose such as a jury might be, or a public committee.

The disciples and Paul used the word 'Ekklesia' when referring to Christians throughout the new testament and not *'Kuriakos'*.

You have my full permission to go through your entire new testament and wherever you find the word *'church'* replace it with the words *'elected and called out people'*. *

Now that we know better how the wording should read we can see that Jesus said to Peter:

So I tell you, you are Peter. And I will build my 'called out and elected ones' on this rock. The power of death will not be able to defeat my 'called out and elected ones'.

Matthew 16:18 ERV

Jesus was using a play on words here.

The name *'Peter'* when translated into English means *'rock'*. If you have been to Greece and are familiar with the Greek language you might recognise it as *'Petra'*.

OK so clearly Jesus wasn't talking about putting up a building on top of Peter so what does that verse mean?

To understand that we need to go back and read the verse in context with the conversation that Jesus was having with his disciples.

Jesus had been asking his disciples who they thought that he was.

Let's place the verses here so that you can read them.

The conversation begins in Matthew 16.13.

Jesus went to the area of Caesarea Philippi.

He said to his followers, "Who do people say I am ?"

They answered, "Some people say you are John the Baptizer. Others say you are Elijah. And some say you are Jeremiah or one of the prophets."

Then Jesus said to his followers, "And who do you say I am?"

Simon Peter answered, "You are the Messiah, the Son of the living God."

Jesus answered, "You are blessed, Simon son of Jonah. No one taught you that.

My Father in heaven showed you who I am.

So I tell you, you are Peter. And I will build my church on this rock. The power of death will not be able to defeat my church.

Matthew 16:13-18 ERV

The disciples had told Jesus who others thought that he was and then Peter suddenly had a flash of inspiration, a revelation of who Jesus really was!

Peter blurted out, 'You are the Messiah! The son of the Living God!

Jesus realised that no one had told Peter this news. It had been a revelation, a thought process direct from God.

And so Jesus told him so and went on to say that it was on this *'Rock'* (of revelation - God's thoughts) that His 'elected and called out people' would be built.

We are God's elected and called out people. We are God's building. We are His Holy Temple which is built without hands.

We are Gods dwelling place which is built on the 'rock' of revelation.

It is us, His elected, called out people that Jesus was referring to - not some old building made of stone.

We are being built and bonded together by God's personal revelation to each one of us.

It is on this rock of revelation that we are being built.

Some people might tell you that, 'it's not the building but the people who are the church'.

You can now reply, in the kindest way, 'Jesus didn't even talk about the church', we are not *'Kuriakos'*, we are *'Ekklesia'*, we are God's 'elected and called out people'.

We have seen that the word 'church' (*'Kuriakos'*) means to be under or belonging to a lord.

Who is the lord that the church is under?

At this time many are feeling uneasy within the present 'church systems' for very good reasons.

God's Spirit is causing uneasiness in His people. There is dissatisfaction within those church systems that have been established by man.

Some attempt to quell that uneasy feeling by rearranging the chairs or by inventing new ways of organising the services - 'messy church' is one such attempt. Some organise coffee mornings or invite the TV producers in.

These are all symptoms of the unease within the church systems - something doesn't feel quite right.

People wonder, "Where is God"?

God is calling many out of these man made systems in order to establish His reign in our lives.

I would encourage any who are feeling uneasy to come out of that place. You are being nudged by Spirit at this time in order to come out and under His own Lordship.

We were never intended to come under the lordship of anyone else.

There are no go between leaders, pastors or priests in God's Kingdom, only a one to one relationship with God the Spirit in union with all of God's children.

The true Lord is calling us out right now. Don't linger any longer under the lordship of someone else.

Then I heard another voice from heaven saying, "Come out of her, my people, lest you take part in her sins, lest you share in her plagues; for her sins are heaped high as heaven, and God has remembered her iniquities.

Revelation 18:4-5 ESV

We will talk about this verse more fully another time.

I love that last line that we read in Mathew:

Jesus said:-

"The gates of hell shall not prevail against my elected and called out people".

Matthew 16:18 KJV

- There are in fact only two occasions where the word *'Kuriakos'* was used by the writers of the new testament and on neither occasion was the word *'church'* implied.
- These are in 1 Cor. 11:20 when referring to the Passover, the meal that 'belongs to the Lord'. And also in Rev. 1:10. When referring to 'the Lords day'. The writer was referring to a day that 'belonged to a lord'. i.e. it was a day of importance – one to remember. Not a particular day of the week but one of note because it was dedicated to a Lord (a Roman god).
- Elsewhere in the Bible the word. *'Ekklesia'* is used 112 times purposefully because the writers had a specific meaning in mind.

Nowhere in the whole volume of the Bible is there anywhere a reference or concept of the word *'church'* as we have been taught it.

The writers of the New Testament had no thought at all of the church systems that exists today.

Christians at this time and for long after would meet in small groups in each others houses.

Even when there were hundreds or thousands within an area they would meet in small groups of family and close friends - many of them scattered around an area.

When we read letters that are addressed to the elected and called out ones in an area in the Bible, the letters written would have been read by those small groups and then passed around from person to person.

We imagine them being read out to a large congregation because that is what we know of the present day set up but then that wasn't the case and for good reason.

The reason is that there is relationship going on within a small group.

God builds His Kingdom upon relationships - not on the basis of going to church.

God does things with a small group He does not seem to do with a large one.

Everyone can be a part and participate within a small group.

Small groups are infectious and effective.

Peer to peer teaching and encouragement and sharing of revelation happens within a small group.

Just to emphasise how relevant small groups are I will note below what Paul wrote to an area where there are hundreds of Christians in Corinth.

This is what I mean, my friends.

When you meet for worship, one person has a hymn, another a teaching, another a revelation from God, another a message in strange tongues, and still another the explanation of what is said.

Everything must be of help to the elect.

If someone is going to speak in strange tongues, two or three at the most should speak, one after the other, and someone else must explain what is being said. But if no one is there who can explain, then the one who speaks in strange tongues must be quiet and speak only to himself and to God.

Two or three who are given God's message should speak, while the others are to judge what they say. But if someone sitting in the meeting receives a message from God, the one who is speaking should stop.

All of you may proclaim God's message, one by one, so that everyone will learn and be encouraged.

The gift of proclaiming God's message should be under the speaker's control,

1 Corinthians 14:26-32 GNT

Paul is talking here about the need for some order when they meet up and for it not to be a time of confusion. But it seems to be clear that he is addressing people who he expects to be meeting with just a few in the group so that they are all able to take part.

Paul's letter would have been copied and then passed from group to group and person to person.

As we have said earlier, nowhere in the whole volume of the Bible is there anywhere a reference or concept of the word *'church'* as we know it. It simply did not exist.

Now that's strange isn't it?

So, the question has to be asked, where does the idea of church come from?

If it wasn't from God in heaven; if it wasn't from Jesus on earth and it definitely wasn't from angels or the apostles or any disciples, where on earth has this church idea come from?

I will give you a brief but definite answer to that question right now but you will find that I have elaborated on this question elsewhere as well.

There are only two sources of information for mankind. One source is God and the other comes from the enemy.

Both sources are often trickled into our consciousness via third parties.

'Church' - *Kuriakos'* began during the reign of the Roman Emperor Constantine.

There had been some deterioration before this time: there were some regional divisions, bishops had been appointed to look after various groupings and also leaders had been chosen, all of which had been done in opposition to the teachings of Jesus.

"But you must not be called 'Teacher.' You are all equal as brothers and sisters. You have only one Teacher. And don't call anyone on earth 'Father.' You have one Father. He is in heaven. And you should not be called 'Master.' You have only one Master, the Messiah. Whoever serves you like a servant is the greatest among you.

Matthew 23:8-11 ERV

We have also read the teachings of Paul:

So, brothers and sisters, what should you do?

When you meet together, one person has a song, another has a teaching, and another has a new truth from God.

One person speaks in a different language, and another interprets that language. The purpose of whatever you do should be to help everyone grow stronger in faith.

And only two or three prophets should speak. The others should judge what they say.

And if a message from God comes to someone who is sitting, the first speaker should be quiet.

1 Corinthians 14:26, 29-30 ERV

Paul clearly expected Christians to be equal and contribute equally as Spirit prompted them. The only leadership for Christians should be the Spirit of God.

It was, however, the Emperor Constantine who managed to virtually wipe out all knowledge of the teachings of Jesus and His disciples.

'The people of the way' as we were known during the 1st century or *'the Ecclesia'* as Jesus has called us were dealt a destructive blow by Constantine.

Constantine reigned in the period C.E. 272 – 337.

In order to cut down on the highly expensive and time consuming costs of settling squabbles between rival tribes, religions and peoples Constantine decided to set up a new world religion that everyone in his Kingdom must either follow or be killed.

Constantine's mother was a Christian and so he had an idea of how Christians behaved - peaceably, not causing trouble, not rebelling against authorities etc.

Therefore Constantine's new world religion was based upon the Christian theme. It wasn't rooted in Spirit it was a counterfeit religion.

At the same time Constantine outlawed any group meeting in houses - the Christian way of meeting up in order to share what God was doing was made illegal.

People were ordered instead to meet in church buildings that were imitations of the pagan temples that were so prevalent in the Roman Empire at the time.

He also created an elite group of priests and clergy in order to control the new congregations.

Church was born.

The elected called out ones eventually became nothing more than spectators within a counterfeit world system.

Very little has changed within this counterfeit religion for two thousand years, even to this day.

There have been brief outbursts of revival, reformation, and new moves of God's Spirit among those who have sought Him.

These moves have generally ended with the emergence of yet another denomination - another split in the unity of God's people.

However, God is calling His chosen people out of these counterfeit church systems today.

A new generation of elected and called out ones are appearing on the earth.

Something is happening in God's Kingdom.

If you feel stifled where you are then I urge you to get involved in what God is doing now. This is no time to hang around. God is on the move.

But you might be sitting there thinking to yourself, "well that's an interesting fact but why does it matter how we meet up?

What is the difference between going to church or meeting in small groups? We are all God's children at the end of the day, aren't we"?

In part you are correct. We certainly are all God's children if we have a relationship with Jesus no matter how we come together or even if we don't meet up with others at all.

This is why we need to keep open all areas of relationship with others who might meet in a different way to us. We don't want to create any further divisions in His body do we? And by keeping open relationships with others no matter how we might disagree on some things we keep the unity of His body which is crucial bearing in mind what we know about how God's Kingdom is made up and also, as we will learn later, the imminent return of Jesus.

I have indicated earlier in this chapter some of the negative aspects that had started to affect the way that Jesus' called out people met together not long after the first and second century - divisions amongst groups were developing and some leaders and even bishops had been appointed over geographical areas in opposition to the teaching of Jesus.

Jesus said:

"But you must not be called 'Teacher.' You are all equal as brothers and sisters. You have only one Teacher. And

don't call anyone on earth 'Father.' You have one Father. He is in heaven.

And you should not be called 'Master.' You have only one Master, the Messiah.

"It will be bad for you teachers of the law and you Pharisees! You are hypocrites! You close the way for people to enter God's kingdom. You yourselves don't enter, and you stop those who are trying to enter.

"It will be bad for you teachers of the law and you Pharisees! You are hypocrites. You travel across the seas and across different countries to find one person who will follow your ways.

When you find that person, you make him worse than you are. And you are so bad that you belong in hell!

Matthew 23:8-10, 13, 15 ERV

Those last two paragraphs are so true, aren't they? How many missionary outreaches have sadly ended this way?

The words that Jesus spoke when He was on earth are just as true and valid today.

It isn't looking good for anyone who raises themselves or allows others to raise them up to a position of that type of leadership, pastorship or clergy in a church system does it?

God's Kingdom isn't organised the same way as the world organises its business.

Jesus said that we are all equal and we are not to call any person, man or woman, 'master' or 'father' or to give anyone any title that raises them up above the others.

We have only one Father and He is in heaven.

Each one of us has access to Him and we have His Spirit.

Each one of us can hear His voice for him or herself. We have no need of intermediaries.

Of course we need to check with other mature Christians that what we are hearing from God is right, that is the purpose of there being mature believers around.

Whilst we are growing up we need spiritual adults around us to guide and teach.

Those who are more mature should not see themselves as leaders though or allow themselves to be esteemed as such.

In fact as we can see from Jesus words - any person who acts as an intermediary is effectively doing so in rebellion to God.

Paul gave us a clear understanding of the work of the Spirit with us when we meet up in the section I quoted earlier in 1. Corinthians 14.26

When we come together everyone of us has something to bring. (para).

Paul also highlighted the problem that occurs within church systems when there are leaders or pastors or clergy or fathers or even a leadership team, there are many variations in the way that men stand in the place that is reserved for God alone. (let's keep it simple and name them all 'leaders').

This is what Paul wrote:

You have had enough time that by now you should be teachers. But you need someone to teach you again the first lessons of God's teaching.

You still need the teaching that is like milk. You are not ready for solid food.

Anyone who lives on milk is still a baby and is not able to understand much about living right. But solid food is for people who have grown up. From their experience they have learned to see the difference between good and evil.

Hebrews 5:12-14 ERV

Paul isn't suggesting that teachers have a particular place or are any more important than other gifts. He is explaining that the people that he was writing to should be past the stage of being taught in that way, they should be mature enough to learn for themselves and to be teaching others.

They were still babies and were not growing up.

This is a problem that occurs in church systems - this is why the enemy established church systems and raised up leaders.

People within them generally do not grow up to become mature and useful in the Kingdom - they tend to remain as babies, dependent upon a leader to feed them.

This is exactly where the enemy wants them.

Week after week they take their places in the pews to listen to whatever the 'leader' has to say and then return home without having learnt how to receive from God in order to give to others around them.

They remain babies living on milk when they ought to be learning to become mature - able to give from God themselves.

The life of God, if there is any, is ministered by the leader instead of by each other.

Very rarely does the Spirit have the opportunity to speak or act through others and so the congregation never learns to hear God for themselves - they never interact or operate as the body of Christ ought to. There is no need for them to do so.

It will always be left to the designated leader to come up with the next bright idea - to organise the barbeque, run the next outreach, organise the rally or tea party and so on.

The fact that the leader gets paid to do this job makes matters so much worse.

The leader who receives a salary then feels obliged to carry out all of these duties whether God has asked them to or not. The leader too is trapped within the church system.

This is not how it should be.

Why do we pay people a salary in order to carry out something that God has expressly forbidden us to do?

Does this look like something we should be thinking about?

Remember the anointing of King Saul?

God warned the people what would happen if they appointed a leader over them in place of God.

This is exactly the situation that the church system is now.

A secondary but inevitable outcome of this system is the growth of the church power base.

Where a charismatic leader is appointed, the church becomes popular. The Christian leader pulls in the crowds.

Money is accumulated and finance becomes the ruling factor as the church becomes larger.

Within certain denominations the old mosaic law of tithing has been reintroduced in order to support the structure that they have created.

Tithing was a system whereby the Israelites gave a tenth of their income in order to support the priests within the temple worship system that Moses established.

Tithing and the old Mosaic Law has no basis within God's new covenant with man but we will discuss this at another time.

In these manmade and man centred church systems God tends to leave man to his own devices and the church is led mainly by one charismatic leader after another. The church multiplies as a result of its popularity and other similar churches are planted elsewhere.

This movement quickly becomes a denomination and sets itself apart from others.

The power base is established. Leaders and singers alike are worshipped by the congregation.

The congregation themselves remain as babies however, wrapped up in a weekly dose of entertainment, never learning how to grow up to become mature Christians themselves.

This is the pattern of big business in the world - the same spirit rules in both situations.

God is calling us out of these manmade systems.

We are not here in God's Kingdom in order to climb a ladder of accomplishment or to create our own power base or to live in the shadow of another person.

Ah but you might say, "What about the gift of leadership in the book of Romans 12.8 and also in 1 Thessalonians 5.12?"

The Greek word that is used in relation to the gift of leadership in the bible is those passages and elsewhere where leadership is discussed is *'proistemi'.*

Proistemi is a word that is linked with caring and mentoring, assisting and protecting.

It is a gift that is or should be exhibited by all of us for each other and not by one or two overseers.

It is a gift that is more in the nature of a father - son relationship than the way it is used in churches of today.

The same word – *Proistemi,* is used in 1 Timothy 3.5 where Paul is saying, *"if someone isn't able to care for (Proistemi) his own family then how will he care for others in the church?.*

Proistemi is about individuals caring for each other in a fatherly manner and not in the way that it usually used in the church. .

The Kingdom of God is all about building relationships with each other. Not lording it over others.

God is looking for a people who have an ear for His voice and want to become mature people in His Kingdom.

God is looking for a people who are able to grow to become fathers and mothers - to have spiritual children of their own - People who want to grow in His image; who are able to multiply and not to simply live on milk that is spoon fed from the pulpit.

Jesus said to Peter:

These are the people who will pull down the very gates of hell itself.

'The elect of God'.

Are we one of these?

Eternity

Have you ever thought about eternity?

Where does it start? And when does it end?

Eternity is the place where God lives.

He is from 'everlasting until everlasting'. It says so in psalm 103.

Our God is a God of extremes. In the same psalm it says that *He loves us as high as the heavens are from the earth.* That's a long way isn't it?

It also says in the same psalm that if we have come into His Kingdom then *He has put our sins away from us as far as the north is from the south!*

That seems like an impossibly long distance to me!

So how do we measure eternity?

We can't, can we? It is a dimension that is outside both time and space.

That is where God lives!

I will give you another impossible thing to imagine. God is invisible!

Can you imagine such an amazing God who is invisible?

How can we think about someone who is invisible?

We can only really compare Him to the things that we are aware of - the things that we know about.

God is far outside of our understanding. In that way He is unknowable.

We only get a glimpse of Him by reading about His interaction with people and by looking at Jesus' life and by our relationship with Spirit - who is God.

Anyway, I digress. We were talking about eternity weren't we?

Eternity is another dimension that we have trouble coming to terms with. It isn't something that we have experienced before and yet God wants us to have a mind set with a view of eternity in our own lives.

When we came into God's Kingdom we became people who are designed for eternity.

Eternity for God's new creation begins the moment we come into His Kingdom.

We are eternal!

Our bodies may get old and shrivel and shrink but the essential that is us, if we are born again of Spirit, will live into eternity with God.

Isn't that an amazing fact?

If we really understood our own relationship with eternity I think that we would probably behave very differently in this life.

We talked earlier about being Overcomers, didn't we?

We are all living in God's Kingdom with the purpose of overcoming the enemy.

We were born of the Spirit in order to pull down the strongholds of the enemy: to break down the very gates of hell itself.

That is what God has designed and called us to do, each one of us.

God has already placed in our lives the strongholds that we need to attack and has also given us the ability in unity with Him to pull them down.

Paul puts it like this:

God has made us what we are. In Christ Jesus, God made us new people so that we would spend our lives doing the good things he had already planned for us to do.

Ephesians 2:10

Paul also talks about eternity when he writes to the Corinthian Christians:

We must all stand before Christ to be judged. Everyone will get what they should. They will be paid for whatever they did—good or bad—when they lived in this earthly body.

2 Corinthians 5:10 ERV

Paul clearly wanted to be judged for doing good!

Paul spent a long time persecuting Christians before he had a revelation of Jesus as his Lord. But, Paul knows he will not be judged for that time. Those sins have been forgiven and forgotten by God. It is the years he has spent as a child of God that will be judged.

It is the same for us today.

We will not be judged for the time we did not know God. If we have come into God's Kingdom those years have been forgiven already

It is what we have done in the years, many or few, which we have had available during our life as a child of God which will be recounted on the Day of Judgement.

We will not be punished for that life as it is not a judgement of punishment, but we will receive God's assessment of what we have done.

Some will receive a "Well done" and crowns of glory.

Others might realise too late that they have wasted their time and have nothing to show. How sad for these people.

Some will receive responsibility to serve as rulers with Jesus of cities. Others will receive lesser accolades. What will we receive on that day?

The fact is that Paul is so convinced of the reality of these things that he is prepared to face death daily.

His future life in eternity is worth so much more than the temporary discomfort of this life.

Does the excitement and reality of eternity grip us so much that we do not have too much interest in this world? I pray that it does.

Is eternity for all?

We have seen that for Christians there will be a time of judgement of all that we have done since coming into God's Kingdom.

For some it will be a 'well done' and a crown. There will be various responsibilities for those who have overcome the enemy whilst reigning for one thousand years with Jesus.

Overcomers will also be gathered in to become the 'bride of Christ'.

There will be a wedding feast.

At the wedding feast there will be the bride of Christ and also guests and others.

These will not be reigning with Jesus for one thousand years but will have a place with him in eternity.

But what of those who reject the offer of redemption?

What about the people who don't listen to the Good News? The ones who prefer to live this life without God?

We are told that there will be a great sadness for them

In Isaiah we find that they simply do not rise again - an eternal death. Now that is a very long time - and so sad. What a waste!

The [wicked] dead will not live [again], the spirits of the dead will not rise and return; Therefore You have punished and destroyed them, And You have wiped out every memory of them [every trace of them].

ISAIAH 26:14 AMP

That is such a sad fate for anyone isn't it?

God doesn't want this to happen to a single soul which is why He sent Jesus in order to offer a free way back to God.

Redemption can only come via Jesus.

There is another group that we haven't talked about - the enemy and the fallen angels - demons that rebelled against God and were thrown out of heaven.

What happens to them?

The enemy himself likes to promote the idea that he is somehow in control of hell. What a lie. Let's see his fate.

"Then He will say to those on His left, 'Leave Me, you cursed ones, into the eternal fire which has been prepared for the devil and his angels (demons);

MATTHEW 25:41 AMP

Then the Devil, who deceived them, was thrown into the lake of fire and sulphur, where the beast and the false prophet had already been thrown; and they will be tormented day and night forever and ever.

Revelation 20:10 GNT

The sea gave up the dead who were in it. Death and Hades gave up the dead who were in them. All these people were judged by what they had done. And Death and Hades were thrown into the lake of fire. This lake of fire is the second death.

Revelation 20:13-14 ERV

The enemy - Satan, and his demons will be thrown into a lake of fire.

That sounds pretty final for him to me. So much for the lie that promotes him being in charge of anything.

It appears also from the above verse that finally even death and Hades itself will be thrown into the lake of fire.

What does eternity hold on store for you?

Restoration

There is a broad expectation in the world today and also amongst some Christians that the world is going down the tube.

Negativity is everywhere. We look for the next disaster. Things are going from bad to worse.

The world limps from one crisis to another.

The end of the world is just around the corner.

Well is it?

Let's see what God thinks of that shall we?

When Jesus came to earth, one of his purposes was the restoration of His creation.

When Adam rebelled against God the whole of creation fell into an ever worsening sinful state. The enemy made good use of the short time that he has to bring about the destruction of mankind. But he failed and will continue to fail.

God's heart ached as he longed for His creation to be redeemed.

Jesus was and is the answer.

Did Jesus succeed? Was his victory over the enemy fully accomplished?

Or has God washed his hands of the earth and mankind and Is He just waiting for its destruction?

The truth is that Jesus came in order to restore all things.

We don't read too much in the Bible about God's creation other than how it interacts with His relationship and dealings with mankind.

We are told how and why and when the entire universe was created and that it was God who spoke it into existence.

The creation of everything appears to have one purpose and that is to support mankind in various ways.

Isn't that amazing? All of creation was designed and planned in order to support and please you and me!

Mankind likes to think that we own it, and can divide it up into neat ownership packages from the dividing of nations right down to our own square patch of property that we call home but in fact it all belongs to God. We are simply stewards and we will be held responsible one day for the way that we have looked after it.

In fact we can read in the book of psalms the very same thing:

The earth and everything on it belong to the Lord. The world and all its people belong to him. He built the earth on the water. He built it over the rivers.

Psalms 24:1-2 ERV

And as if to confirm the truth of this Paul, when talking about what foods to eat, also writes:

You can eat it, "because the earth and everything in it belong to the Lord."

1 Corinthians 10:26 ERV

The earth and the whole universe belong to God.

The prophet Isaiah had a lot to say about how God will one day bring restoration to His creation and also to the people who belong to Him.

We can read about both the blessings that are to come to God's people and the land and the curses that will inevitably fall on his enemies in the book of Isaiah.

I have noted a couple of small sections below:

"No longer will babies die when only a few days old.

No longer will adults die before they have lived a full life.

No longer will people be considered old at one hundred!

Only the cursed will die that young!

In those days people will live in the houses they build and eat the fruit of their own vineyards.

Unlike the past, invaders will not take their houses and confiscate their vineyards.

For my people will live as long as trees, and my chosen ones will have time to enjoy their hard-won gains.

They will not work in vain, and their children will not be doomed to misfortune.

For they are people blessed by the Lord , and their children, too, will be blessed.

I will answer them before they even call to me.

While they are still talking about their needs, I will go ahead and answer their prayers!

Isaiah 65:20-24 NLT

It appears from reading that fourth line that this will be a time when all people are living on the earth.

And also:

You will live in joy and peace.

The mountains and hills will burst into song, and the trees of the field will clap their hands!

Where once there were thorns, cypress trees will grow.

Where nettles grew, myrtles will sprout up. These events will bring great honour to the Lord's name; they will be an everlasting sign of his power and love."

Isaiah 55:12-13 NLT

Matthew also writes about what Jesus said about restoration.

Jesus said to them, "I assure you and most solemnly say to you, in the renewal [that is, the Messianic restoration and regeneration of all things] when the Son of Man sits on His glorious throne, you [who have followed Me, becoming My disciples] will also sit on twelve thrones, judging the twelve tribes of Israel.

MATTHEW 19:28 AMP

Jesus also taught his disciples and us to pray earnestly for God's government to rule in earth in the same way that it does in Heaven.

may your Kingdom come; may your will be done on earth as it is in heaven.

Matthew 6:10 GNT

Did you read that correctly?

Jesus told His disciples and us to pray towards God's will being done on earth!

That is God's Kingdom on earth.

Peter also spoke about the restoration of all things soon after Jesus had gone back to heaven:

For he must remain in heaven until the time for the final restoration of all things, as God promised long ago through his holy prophets.

Acts of the Apostles 3:21

Paul writes about all of creation groaning in pain, just waiting for the children of God to be revealed.

Let's read what he said:

Everything that God made is waiting with excitement for the time when he will show the world who his children are.

The whole world wants very much for that to happen. Everything God made was allowed to become like something that cannot fulfil its purpose.

That was not its choice, but God made it happen with this hope in view: That the creation would be made free from ruin—that everything God made would have the same freedom and glory that belong to God's children.

We know that everything God made has been waiting until now in pain like a woman ready to give birth to a child.

Romans 8:19-22 ERV

Paul is explaining that all of creation is groaning in pain, since sin entered the world and left its mark on everything.

The whole of creation is just waiting for something to happen!

What great event is creation waiting for?

For the children of God to be revealed to the world - vs. 19.

Waiting for the bride

So, who are the children of God?

Well that would be you and me and all who have come into God's Kingdom. Isn't this exciting?

We are the children of God!

Those children of God who are known to Him as Overcomers are called the Bride of Christ.

It says so in the book of Revelation:

Let us rejoice and be happy and give God glory! Give God glory, because the wedding of the Lamb has come.

And the Lamb's bride has made herself ready.

Fine linen was given to the bride for her to wear. The linen was bright and clean." (The fine linen means the good things that God's holy people did.)

Revelation 19:7-8 ERV

So, when might this great event occur?

When will the children of God be revealed to the world?

It looks like this big event will happen when the Lamb marries the Bride.

The Lamb is the Lord Jesus and the Bride, as we have already seen is us - the elected and called out ones - the Overcomers.

This is when the marriage feast will be.

So, the whole of creation is just waiting for the wedding?

Yes, it seems so.

So, what is preventing any of this happening straight away- like now or tomorrow?

Will Jesus come to get His Bride any time now?

Let's find out shall we?

We will read again what it says in the book of Revelation:

Let us rejoice and be happy and give God glory! Give God glory, because the wedding of the Lamb has come. And the Lamb's bride has made herself ready.

Fine linen was given to the bride for her to wear.

The linen was bright and clean." (The fine linen means the good things that God's holy people did.)

Revelation 19:7-8 ERV.

We find that the Bride to be has 'made herself ready' and 'clothed herself in fine linen'.

Fine linen is a reference to the good deeds of the Bride - which is us - the elected and called out ones, having prepared ourselves and being in a state of readiness for the Bridegroom.

Can you imagine a Bridegroom waiting for the Bride to arrive at the wedding and the Bride turns up in ragged clothes, unwashed and dirty?

It wouldn't happen would it?

How ready and prepared for the Bridegroom do we think that the Bride is at the moment?

Shall we look around and take stock?

It is a sad picture isn't it.

Everywhere in the Kingdom of God we see divisions and squabbles.

We find people who won't talk to other people, we find that the majority of Christians haven't got a clue what living in God's Kingdom is all about - we have never been taught.

We find groups of downtrodden, helpless, weak Christians who are unable or unwilling to rise from the yokes that they are under. We find unhealthy addiction, pornography, deceit and all manner of evil things occurring amongst leaders and youngsters alike.

Does this picture give you a vision of a healthy beautiful Bride? A bride who has adorned herself with fine linen? One who has risen victorious over the enemy?

If these people are a part of the Bride then I think that Jesus the Lamb who is the Bridegroom will be waiting a little longer for His Bride to prepare herself, don't you?

But perhaps some of those people above aren't going to be a part of the bride.

They certainly don't sound or look as if they are preparing for the groom, do they?

Perhaps there are others who are willing to be obedient and are ready and prepared right now to be the Bride?

If this is the case then Jesus might come at any time for His Bride.

Notice that it isn't God, or Jesus who prepares the Bride - It is the Bride who prepares herself as any Bride might do in preparation for a wedding.

So, if all of creation is in pain waiting for the children of God to be shown to the world as the Bride of Christ, when will she be prepared? How long must we wait?

The answer to that question is really lying in our own hands.

How excited are we about being the Bride of Christ?

How much do we want to build that relationship with Spirit and to join with others in overcoming the enemy?

How much do we want to see God's will being carried out on earth as it is in heaven?

How well are we restoring those bad relationships?

It is our own desire, our own prayers, our own ability to be obedient and effective in God's Kingdom that will bring about the preparedness of the Bride.

We are God's plan A. God has no other plan.

The restoration of all of creation is our responsibility and it is our responsibility now.

But look! There is good news!

Look around again and we will see a new generation of people rising up and wanting to serve Jesus.

There are people with hearts that are turned towards Jesus:- wanting to learn how to walk in faith in partnership with the Spirit of God.

There is a burning desire amongst us to put away all that which is wood, hay and stubble - all that will be burnt up in the fire and to learn to build upon the rock that is Jesus.

Let's not keep Jesus waiting any longer.

We have work to do.

Who we are

I wrote a little about who we now are since coming into God's Kingdom in my last book *'Journey into Life'*. I have been asked to expand upon this theme.

There are many people who have come into God's Kingdom and have no teaching to reveal who we have now become. So what is it that we have come into?

Where do we belong?

What is our purpose?

Let's try to fill in some gaps shall we.

I have referred to who we are many times throughout this book but let's just sit back and take a thorough stock of what or rather who we are now in Christ, shall we?

We are redeemed - we were destined to die but Jesus has paid the price for us.

We are sanctified because of the blood of Jesus. This means that we are made holy and acceptable to God - we are able to walk right into the presence of God unafraid and unashamed. Isn't that amazing?

We are made a new creation - when we went through the baptism of water God himself declared us to be His own children - we became a part of God's family and more than that even - God's Spirit made His home with us - we actually became one with God.

The bible says we became a new creation.

When Paul wrote to the Christians at Corinth he said this:

Therefore, if anyone is in Christ, he is a new creation; old things have passed away; behold, all things have become new.

II Corinthians 5:17 NKJV

Because we are now one with Spirit we are also one with God the Father and also one with Jesus.

We were spiritually dead because of all we had done against him.

But he gave us new life together with Christ. (You have been saved by God's grace.)

Yes, it is because we are a part of Christ Jesus that God raised us from death.

Ephesians 2:5-6 ERV

We do not live under anything or anyone any longer; we are born to be seated with Him in the heavenlies!

We live no longer in condemnation, sentenced to death as a sinner but we live as a redeemed, Spirit filled, new creation.

We have moved into a new Kingdom.

There is nothing in the old Kingdom that has any hold on us any more - we are set free from the old - the new has come.

Together, united, we are a body. Just as a body has different parts – a leg, an arm, a foot and a heart – so does the Body of Christ. We are different parts of His Body, with a different purpose. I might be a leg, you might be an arm, someone else might be a foot or a heart. We are called to work together as the body of Christ.

Paul wrote to the Christians at Corinth about this:

A person has only one body, but it has many parts.

Yes, there are many parts, but all those parts are still just one body.

Christ is like that too.

Some of us are Jews and some of us are not; some of us are slaves and some of us are free. But we were all baptized to become one body through one Spirit. And we were all given the one Spirit.

And a person's body has more than one part. It has many parts.

The foot might say, "I am not a hand, so I don't belong to the body." But saying this would not stop the foot from being a part of the body.

The ear might say, "I am not an eye, so I don't belong to the body." But saying this would not make the ear stop being a part of the body.

If the whole body were an eye, it would not be able to hear.

If the whole body were an ear, it would not be able to smell anything. If each part of the body were the same part, there would be no body.

But as it is, God put the parts in the body as he wanted them. He made a place for each one.

So there are many parts, but only one body. The eye cannot say to the hand, "I don't need you!" And the head cannot say to the foot, "I don't need you!"

No, those parts of the body that seem to be weaker are actually very important. And the parts that we think are not worth very much are the parts we give the most care to. And we give special care to the parts of the body that we don't want to show. The more beautiful parts don't need this special care. But God put the body together and gave more honour to the parts that need it.

God did this so that our body would not be divided.

God wanted the different parts to care the same for each other.

If one part of the body suffers, then all the other parts suffer with it. Or if one part is honoured, then all the other parts share its honour.

All of you together are the body of Christ. Each one of you is a part of that body.

1 Corinthians 12:12-27 ERV

Also in his letter to the Christians at Ephesus:

No, we will speak the truth with love.

We will grow to be like Christ in every way.

He is the head, and the whole body depends on him.

All the parts of the body are joined and held together, with each part doing its own work. This causes the whole body to grow and to be stronger in love.

Ephesians 4:15-16 ERV

Jesus is the head of the body - the body will not function well unless it is rightly connected to the head who is Jesus.

We also need to find and connect to the joints that God has created for us

God places those people in our life as we build our relationship with Him.

Just to add to that, in case it is not clear - Jesus is the head, we are the body - together and complete we are one new man.

Can you imagine that?

God loved us so much that He has designed things so that we, together, actually become one new, spiritual man with Jesus!

This is who we are in Christ. It really is astounding!

God has also given us gifts.

When we came into God's Kingdom God gave us spiritual gifts to use.

Some are for building others up, some are for praising Him, and some are for the benefit of others outside of His Kingdom in order to bring them inside. Some are for our own personal use.

There are gifts of healing, teaching, prophesy, praise, gifts of speaking in an unknown language, the ability to interpret unknown languages, gifts that enable us to recognise demons, and the ability to perform miracles. There are gifts of evangelism, gifts of looking after people - all manner of gifts have been given for the purpose of building God's Kingdom, which includes us.

We may have one particular gift or we may have many gifts.

God's Spirit will help us to use them effectively.

We are a supernatural being. We are born for eternity.

We are designed to overcome. In partnership with God's Spirit we are able to pull down the very gates of hell itself.

As we read earlier, Jesus said to His disciples:

And I tell you that you are Peter, and on this rock I will build my 'ecclesia', and the gates of Hades will not overcome it.

Matthew 16:18 NIV

You are more than a conqueror.

Yet in all these things we are more than conquerors and gain an overwhelming victory through Him who loved us [so much that He died for us].

ROMANS 8:37 AMP

We have spoken earlier about becoming the Bride of Christ.

Jesus will one day return to claim His Bride who will have prepared herself for the wedding.

Becoming the Bride of Christ is linked with being an overcomer.

In the first few chapters of the book of Revelation we can read about the seven other specific rewards that go with being an overcomer in this life. There is a whole chapter all about overcomers later in this book.

But we are looking at who we are now, aren't we?

We have been chosen by God in order to be brought into the Kingdom of God.

Just think of that! We have been chosen by God Himself- handpicked.

God has elected each one of us to be part of His own chosen and called out people.

We have been bought by the blood of Jesus for a specific purpose.

We are an elect and elite group of people - given superpowers in order to serve Jesus in building God's Kingdom.

Before we were even born God had his eye on us. He knew us when we were still in our mother's womb. God has formed us to be who we are.

As a result of the enemy's influence on us there are often things in our lives that we need to be delivered from.

God knows about these things and as we are obedient and attentive to His word He enables us to be freed.

God is so much in love with you and with me.

We are the apple of His eye!

Can we even imagine a love that compelled God to send His only son to earth to be despised and rejected - to be tortured and killed just for us?

We can walk down the street with our head held high because we are loved and because God is well pleased with us!

God has freed us from all of our anxieties and fears. Death itself no longer has any claim over us - it cannot hold us.

We are made free men and free women. Free not to sin. Free to serve Jesus.

Paul writes to the Christians in Galatia and tells them:

We have freedom now, because Christ made us free. So stand strong in that freedom. Don't go back into slavery again.

Galatians 5:1 ERV

Family

When we went through those waters of baptism, not only did God send His Spirit as a sign of His approval and seal of His ownership of us - we were baptised in His Spirit, but we also were born straight into His own family.

We were born into the family of God. We are not born into God's Kingdom to live alone but to be a part of a family of people- people who God will place into our life in order to help us to help them as well.

God's Kingdom is built upon relationships - our relationship with Spirit first and then with others who also have relationship with Spirit.

As those relationships grow stronger so others will see Jesus rising up in us as a community of people and will want to become a part as well.

Purpose

In this life on earth we are born again in order to be redeemed back to God. We are His possession.

There has been much unhelpful teaching with regards to becoming a Christian.

Many evangelists claim that all a person has to do to become a Christian is to raise a hand in a service, or to say a certain prayer, or to walk down to the front of the pulpit.

Sadly this is not true as we have seen in our previous chapters and read in the Bible.

As a result of this teaching many people who desired to come into God's Kingdom have since died a premature spiritual death for lack of spiritual nourishment - they were never fed, never nurtured and so starved, they fell away discouraged and disappointed.

When I hear people talking about the great evangelical crusades of the fifties and sixties and seventies where millions of people across the globe came to Jesus I look around and wonder where are they all now?

We are born into God's family in order to have relationship with Him and with each other - this is how God's Kingdom is built- this is how we prosper and flourish- this is how we grow and mature and learn how to have spiritual children of our own.

It is through relationship that we are able to be taught and in relationship we, in turn, are able to teach others.

So, let's look at what we are here in God's Kingdom for - what is our purpose today?

There are a couple of pieces of scripture that sum up our primary purpose in God's Kingdom.

The first is advice that Jesus Himself gave to His disciples.

But seek first His kingdom and His righteousness, and all these things will be given to you as well.

Matthew 6:33 NIV

Jesus said that the first thing - our priority, is to seek out how to build God's Kingdom.

The way to do that is to come into God's presence regularly.

Don't be afraid, it is what He wants us to do.

We read that when Jesus was on earth, He loved to sit with the children and teach them.

When I was a child I had a text on my bedroom wall above my bed. It was a picture of Jesus holding a child with other children around watching intently. The text read:

"And Jesus took them up into His arms and fervently blessed them".

Mark 10.16.

What always struck me wasn't the fact that Jesus loved children or even that He blessed them. What I was always fascinated by was the fact that He 'fervently' blessed them.

It was as if He was so delighted in blessing them that He did it with all of His might - Jesus put all that He was into blessing those children.

Today it is exactly the same, God delights in us. When we come into His presence His love is overflowing. He is just over the moon with us and takes enormous pleasure in us all of the time.

We are His children and He always delights in 'fervently' blessing us.

The more time that we spend with Him then the more we will become like Him.

Out of our relationship with Him flow many other things, such as:

- Friendships with others in His Kingdom.
- Amazing responsibilities and jobs to do.
- We receive miraculous provision for our own lives but more than that, we are able to do so much for others as well.

As we spend time with Father, then His love begins to change us - we begin to grow up and become mature sons and daughters.

All of this is called fruit.

Just as fruit grows naturally on a fruit tree without the tree needing to struggle and strain to produce it, in the same way fruit of God's Spirit will naturally begin to be produced in our own lives.

There are all sorts of different fruit in the same way that we have different fruit in the greengrocers shop.

Our spiritual fruit will grow naturally as well.

Paul wrote to the Christians in Galatia about this:

But the fruit of the Spirit is love, joy, peace, forbearance, kindness, goodness, faithfulness, gentleness and self-control. Against such things there is no law.

Galatians 5:22-23 NIV

What we produce will be dependent upon the spiritual gifts that we have and how we use them and also upon the character that we allow God to build in us.

If we are teachable and pliable then God will enable us to produce fruits that display His love.

If we are hard and stubborn then the fruit that we bear will also reflect this.

What does fruit look like?

Fruit can be the things that we do for others. It can be the way that others are able to grow and prosper as a result of things that we say or do.

Fruit can be people that come into God's Kingdom as a result of our lives.

Fruit can be the way that we manage the responsibilities that God places in our lives.

Fruit can be the good behaviour and godliness of the children that we produce.

Fruit can show itself in many different ways and forms.

Fruit may not be immediately visible but can also show itself many years later.

Fruit can be good or it can be bad.

A good tree produces good fruit and a bad tree produces bad fruit.

It is by the fruit that we produce that others can tell what type of person we really are - where our heart lies.

As we go about our lives we plant seeds. Again, seeds are produced and planted without any effort. Our words and actions plant seeds in people's lives. What we say and what we do bears fruit in those lives for good or bad.

Our purpose in this life is to produce good fruit. We do this by spending time with God. As we allow God's Spirit to develop and grow in our lives so the fruit that we produce will grow and prosper.

If we produce good fruit then the Spirit will enable us to produce even more.

I would recommend that we spend much time with Father - to have our roots firmly sunk into His Kingdom so that He is able to water and feed us by His Spirit.

Go and produce plenty of good fruit.

Trust the Lord completely, and don't depend on your own knowledge.

With every step you take, think about what he wants, and he will help you go the right way.

Don't trust in your own wisdom, but fear and respect the Lord and stay away from evil.

If you do this, it will be like a refreshing drink and medicine for your body.

Proverbs 3:5-8 ERV.

Overcomers

I have mentioned the word *overcomer* several times throughout this book - so many times in fact that I thought it might be worth having a chapter all about being an overcomer.

Many people have very little understanding about where we are heading.

This not knowing or not understanding may eventually lead to our missing out on our place in eternity.

Missing out on our place in eternity matters very much.

We read in the Bible that we die because we do not understand the truth.

"My people are destroyed because they have no knowledge.".

Hosea 4:6 ERV

If they obey God and serve him, they live out their lives in peace and prosperity. But if not, they will die in ignorance and cross the stream into the world of the dead.

Job 36:11-12 GNT

He will die for lack of instruction (discipline), And in the greatness of his foolishness he will go astray and be lost.

PROVERBS 5:23 AMP

I have written a little about where we are heading in the chapter called Eternity. Here we will discover more. It is essential to know where we are heading so that we can either turn round and reset our compass or have something to aim at, isn't it?

There is no dispute that we are all heading somewhere – either into an eternity of life or into death.

If we are going to aspire to be overcomer's then we need to learn about overcoming.

 The Bible talks a lot about being an *overcomer* or to use a different phrase, about *'being victorious'* or *'being triumphant'* or *'being a conqueror'*.

I will continue to use the word overcomer.

So that we can trace the true meaning and relevance and consequences through the Bible we will need to know what original Greek word or phrase is used that describe these virtues.

It would be of no use whatsoever if we used one word to describe the achievement and then a different word is used to describe who the award is given to would it?

The Greek word that is used for all of these similar phrases is:

'Nikao'.

Strong's listing no 3528 states:

The word *'Nikao'* means to overpower, overcome or to be victorious.

'Niki' comes from the same verb and means victory.

Of interest to some of you sportier readers – the word *'Nike'* means to be victorious.

The Verb *'Nikaw'* is mentioned no less than 28 times in the New Testament.

Let's have a look at some instances of being able to overcome shall we?

But in all these troubles we have complete victory through God, who has shown his love for us.

Romans 8:37 ERV

Our fight is not against people on earth.

We are fighting against the rulers and authorities and the powers of this world's darkness.

We are fighting against the spiritual powers of evil in the heavenly places.

That is why you need to get God's full armour. Then on the day of evil, you will be able to stand strong.

And when you have finished the whole fight, you will still be standing.

Ephesians 6:12-13 ERV

Great blessings belong to those who are tempted and remain faithful! After they have proved their faith, God will give them the reward of eternal life. God promised this to all people who love him.

James 1:12 ERV

But we thank God who gives us the victory through our Lord Jesus Christ!

1 Corinthians 15:57 ERV

You, dear children, are from God and have overcome them, because the one who is in you is greater than the one who is in the world.

1 John 4:4 NIV

And there are many more like that. Just do a simple search to find out!

The Bible is full of references to our ability to overcome.

It begins to give the impression that perhaps we are not born to be the downtrodden, 'unable to manage' sort of people that we thought we were, doesn't it?

It also reveals that there is a clear distinction between those Christians who do not overcome for whatever reason and those who do overcome.

And He said to me, "It is done! I am the Alpha and the Omega, the Beginning and the End. I will give of the fountain of the water of life freely to him who thirsts. He who overcomes shall inherit all things, and I will be his God and he shall be My son.

Revelation 21:6-7 NKJV

We can see from the above verse that the waters of life are free for all who have eternal life but the tree of life is for overcomers only, we will look at this distinction shortly.

Now there can be various reasons for a Christian not to overcome in this life.

The first might be that the person dies shortly after coming into God's Kingdom as did the thief who was on the cross at the same time as Jesus.

Then Jesus said to him, "I promise you, today you will be with me in paradise."

Luke 23:43 ERV

That person had no time to assess his life or receive teaching but recognized only that he was a sinner and in need of being saved.

Another reason may be that we haven't been taught how to overcome or not be aware that we are brought into His Kingdom in order to overcome.

However, if we are aware of our position and simply can't be bothered or are too involved in the world and all that is going on around us perhaps we should begin to wonder if we are really living in God's Kingdom at all.

There is a whole world of difference between not being able for want of a lack of knowledge and not making any effort.

Faith in God - our willingness to seek His help and our own perseverance will play a big part in whether we are able to overcome or not.

For whatever is born of God overcomes the world. And this is the victory that has overcome the world—our faith. Who is he who overcomes the world, but he who believes that Jesus is the Son of God?

I John 5:4-5 NKJV

It is good to know that we can all become overcomers if we have faith in God.

But do we put that faith into practice?

John 16:33 Jesus said I have overcome the world.

Jesus said that He has already overcome the world - He did that through His death on the cross – when Jesus voluntarily gave His life for us it was in order to redeem us from the consequences of sin. The word *'redeem'* means to buy back.

Jesus bought us back from the consequences of sin, which is certain death. We need to walk into and take hold of the victory that He has already accomplished for us.

It is our choice whether we partake of that victory or not.

Why might we want to be Overcomers?

It is not good for us to be living in slavery to anything.

Jesus came to set us free from slavery – from the dominion of Satan in our life. If we do not rise to take the freedom from slavery that Jesus has provided for us we are denying His gift of life. We are walking back into or remaining under the enemy's dominion. For us, Jesus will have died in vain.

Whilst in the world, before we come into God's Kingdom, we are living under the dominion of Satan.

We lie, we cheat, we are deceitful, we steal, we are ungracious, unfriendly, we are lazy, we are disobedient, rebellious, we are mean, we are selfish, we might be murderers, thieves, abusers and bullies. We collect so many unpleasant characteristics whilst we are in the world.

We might suffer from fears, phobias, and character defects. There are all types of afflictions that the enemy loves to keep us enslaved to

These things can all be left behind when we enter God's Kingdom. Often however we bring our bad habits and vices into God's Kingdom with us. These are things that, under God's stewardship we are able to overcome.

We must overcome these things in order for God's character of Love to begin to rise up within us.

Many of our own characteristics are the very opposite of love.

We are mostly selfish people, looking to achieve our own ends and purposes.

If we happen to be nice to someone along the way then this tends to be despite ourselves rather than us being unselfish.

Our tendency is to be kind in order to receive.

If we honestly think about some of our motivations for the things that we do and say then we will quickly realize this is true.

God enables us to overcome our old sinful nature if we allow Him to.

This is an ongoing process in God's Kingdom but our willingness to change makes the process easier.

As we progress God's selfless love begins to flow into us and from us in increasing measure.

When this begins to occur we not only become Christ like ourselves (Christians) but we also create ripples that affect the people around us.

It is, hopefully, our purpose in this life to become overcomers; to become like Christ. So that the world can see Christ in us.

Or we could just not bother.

That is our choice to make.

One might wonder if we have entered God's Kingdom at all though if our choice is to not bother.

Remember the words of Jesus: *"depart from me you doers of iniquity for I never knew you"*. *Matt. 7:23.*

There are many rewards for us in overcoming that we will enjoy in this life:

- The joy of knowing Jesus and being in fellowship with Him through Spirit.

- The pleasure of being a part of God's Kingdom - enjoying all which God brings into our life.
- A sufficiency of all that we need.
- The fruit that comes as a result of living in harmony with God's Spirit. Love, Joy, peace, patience, tenderness, kindness, goodness, faithfulness and the ability to be in control of our thoughts and actions.

The fruit that the Spirit produces in a person's life is love, joy, peace, patience, kindness, goodness, faithfulness, gentleness, and self-control.

Galatians 5:22-23 ERV

There are also specific rewards for overcomers.

There are at least seven specific rewards that are mentioned that only overcomers will receive.

We will look at them now.

They are promises that are given in the book of revelation.

Rev. 2:7 – 3:21.

1. Overcomers are given to eat of the tree of life.

"He who has an ear, let him hear what the Spirit says to the churches. To him who overcomes I will give to eat from the tree of life, which is in the midst of the Paradise of God." '

Revelation 2:7 NKJV

The tree of life is mentioned eleven times in the Bible; three times in the book of Genesis, four times in the book of proverbs and four times in the book of Revelation.

It is as if God is saying that the tree of life was there at the beginning and will also be there into eternity

The tree of life speaks to us about eternity.

It was the tree of life that Adam and Eve were prevented from eating from after they had rebelled against God. God had no intention of allowing sin to enter into eternity.

2. Overcomers will not be hurt by the second death.

"He who has an ear, let him hear what the Spirit says to the churches. He who overcomes shall not be hurt by the second death." '

Revelation 2:11 NKJV

The second death is the lake of fire where all who refuse to accept God's offer of freedom in this life end.

We read about this in Rev. 21:8

But those who are cowards, those who refuse to believe, those who do terrible things, those who kill, those who sin sexually, those who do evil magic, those who worship idols, and those who tell lies—they will all have a place in the lake of burning sulphur. This is the second death."

Revelation 21:8 ERV

3. Overcomers receive hidden manna a white stone and a new name.

"He who has an ear, let him hear what the Spirit says to the churches. To him who overcomes I will give some of the hidden manna to eat. And I will give him a white stone, and on the stone a new name written which no one knows except him who receives it. " '

Revelation 2:17 NKJV

Hidden manna is sustenance for those who know Jesus.

In the desert the Israelites were given manna to eat. It rained on them from heaven each day except for the Sabbath.

Jesus is our 'living bread' it is His word and presence that sustains us day to day.

Hidden manna is sustenance that only overcomers receive as a result of our endurance and faith.

The white stone is an indication of our innocence.

During Jesus's time when a person was tried for a crime the jury came back with either a white stone or a black stone.

A black stone was an indication of guilt whilst a white stone was an indication of innocence. We receive a white stone with a new name inscribed upon it.

That name will reflect our steadfastness, determination, faith and character through many trials, temptations and victories.

It will indicate where we have succeeded and worked through to complete our course.

That name will endure through all eternity and will be known by our God.

4. Overcomers will receive power over the nations, a rod of iron and the morning star.

And he who overcomes, and keeps My works until the end, to him I will give power over the nations— 'He shall rule them with a rod of iron; They shall be dashed to pieces like the potter's vessels' — as I also have received from My Father; and I will give him the morning star.

Revelation 2:26-28 NKJV

When Jesus returns for His Bride there will be a wedding feast.

We have discussed earlier that the Bride will be those who have overcome in this life.

We have not yet talked about who the guests are or who the friends of the bridegroom at the wedding might be.

This event will herald the start of Jesus' reign over the earth for a period of one thousand years.

Guess who will be reigning with Jesus over the nations for one thousand years? You got it right! – overcomers.

Those who have eternal life but are not overcomers do not rule but wait until the thousand years are over.

The verse above states that we will have 'power over the nations and rule with a rod of iron'.

A 'rod of iron' sounds harsh doesn't it?

When Jesus reigns, He will do so with justice and impartiality.

There will be no more discrimination. No more abuse. No more partiality or injustice.

Jesus' reign will be one of truth and fairness. The reign of Jesus will be one of restoration and completion.

In order to bring restoration, fairness and justice there will be a need, no doubt, for some 'pots to be smashed' - there will be some considerable changes to be made. This is what is meant by ruling with a 'rod of iron'.

The responsibility that we will have in ruling over the nations will be dependent upon the responsibility that we were trusted with and overcame and succeeded with during our life on earth.

It is clear that if we as parents are unable to train or discipline our own children in this life then we will not be given responsibility for the oversight of others.

We can see this principle in action within the parable that Jesus told about those who were trusted with much, much would be given.

The people who have some understanding will be given more. And they will have even more than they need. But those who do not have much understanding will lose even the little understanding that they have.

Matthew 13:12 ERV

We will be responsible for settling matters on earth; for putting things right. This might require some 'smashing of 'clay jars' - Potters vessels.

Some training will no doubt be required.

It also states that we will receive the 'morning star'.

You won't be surprised to learn that this doesn't refer to a newspaper.

Peter talks about The Morning Star. It is a reference to our prophetic nature.

This makes us more sure about what the prophets said. And it is good for you to follow closely what they said, which is like a light shining in a dark place. You have that light until the day begins and the morning star brings new light to your minds.

2 Peter 1:19 ERV

We have the morning star like a light shining into our lives. As we respond to that light shining into the dark places of our being, uncovering hidden sins; as we are willing to allow that light to uncover ungodliness and make us righteous - that light rises to shine in our hearts and minds.

5. White garments and the book of Life.

He who overcomes shall be clothed in white garments, and I will not blot out his name from the Book of Life; but I will confess his name before My Father and before His angels.

Revelation 3:5 NKJV

Overcomers receive white garments and the book of life.

White garments are the clothes of the Bride and relate to her righteous acts. We can connect this verse with what is later written in revelation with regards to the marriage feast itself.

Let us be glad and rejoice and give Him glory, for the marriage of the Lamb has come, and His wife has made herself ready." And to her it was granted to be arrayed in fine linen, clean and bright, for the fine linen is the righteous acts of the saints.

Revelation 19:7-8 NKJV

The book of life is the place where everyone's name is written before that name is blotted out by sin.

But the Lord said to Moses, "The only people I erase from my book are those who sin against me.

Exodus 32:33 ERV

If we want our name to return to that book we need to become overcomers. We can only do that through Jesus.

6. A pillar in the temple of God.

He who overcomes, I will make him a pillar in the temple of My God, and he shall go out no more. I will write on him the name of My God and the name of the city of My God, the New Jerusalem, which comes down out of heaven from My God. And I will write on him My new name.

Revelation 3:12 NKJV

A pillar speaks of our strength. An overcomer is supportive, a person upon whom people lean on.

Overcomers are dependable and trustworthy. A pillar is immovable and as a result of our faith overcomers will not be put off or change course.

The New Jerusalem and the temple that is referred to here are described in Rev. 21.

We are precious to God and will be built into His New Jerusalem. The name of God is to be written into our fabric not because we may become lost but because He is so proud for us to belong to Him.

'I am His and He is mine and His banner over me is Love'.

Song of Solomon 2:4

7. To sit with Jesus on His throne. To reign with Jesus.

To him who overcomes I will grant to sit with Me on My throne, as I also overcame and sat down with My Father on His throne.

Wow! Overcomers get to sit with Jesus on His throne!

The best reward has certainly been saved until the last hasn't it?

This is an overwhelming promise.

Can we imagine reigning with Jesus?

I for one certainly don't want to be considered not quite up to standard on the overcoming scales.

What must it mean to have lived a whole life on this earth with the opportunities that are available to us right now and then for us to be considered not an overcomer?

What possible reason or excuse could we give?

I will add to these yet another verse for our consideration.

In the book of Revelation just before the writer talks about the lake of sulphur we read:

And He said to me, "It is done! I am the Alpha and the Omega, the Beginning and the End. I will give of the fountain of the water of life freely to him who thirsts. He who overcomes shall inherit all things, and I will be his God and he shall be My son.

Revelation 21:6-7 NKJV

It appears that God is saying that all who have eternal life may drink or the fountain of the water of life but overcomers will inherit all things.

There will be others enjoying eternal life, those chosen by God who lived by faith before the birth of Jesus for example and people like the thief on the cross who had no time to overcome.

Possibly children who lost their lives before they were able to make a decision for Jesus are included in this multitude but it is only the overcomers who inherit all things.

I wonder what the 'all things' are?

And also God Himself breaks in to say that *"He will be our God and we will be His son"*.

Just think about all that that statement implies.

This life that we have on earth is so short a time. Who knows when we will be removed from it?

Let's get involved with the things that really do matter.

Let's get involved with the God of creation. What is there to stop us?

A Feast and a Wedding

We have talked about overcomers being the Bride of Christ.

When Jesus returns He will be returning for a glorious Bride – a Bride who has prepared herself by putting on white robes of righteousness.

There will be a feast and a wedding ceremony.

Who will be there?

When Jesus was on earth He often used things that were understood by His listeners to explain His teaching.

One big event that was known and understood and celebrated in those days was the wedding celebration.

The Best Man

John the Baptist also referred to the wedding celebration when talking about Jesus in relation to himself.

The bride always belongs to the bridegroom.

The friend who helps the bridegroom just waits and listens. He is happy just to hear the bridegroom talk.

That's how I feel now. I am so happy that he is here.

John 3:29 ERV

John the Baptist was happy to be the bridegroom's friend or perhaps today we would refer to him as the best man.

In those days it was customary for the friend of the bridegroom to prepare everything in readiness for the wedding.

Mark begins his own narrative on Jesus' life on earth with the words of Isaiah the prophet:

The Good News about Jesus the Messiah, the Son of God, begins with what the prophet Isaiah said would happen.

He wrote: "Listen! I will send my messenger ahead of you. He will prepare the way for you." Malachi 3:1

"There is someone shouting in the desert: 'Prepare the way for the Lord. Make the road straight for him.'" Isaiah 40:3

Mark 1:1-3 ERV

And so it was that John the Baptist came preaching in order to "prepare the way for The Lord".

This is what a true friend of the bridegroom is born for.

We can be sure that John the Baptist will be at the wedding feast performing the duty of a friend of the bridegroom.

The Ten Virgins

Jesus also referred to a wedding when He talked about the wise and the foolish virgins.

I have written the parable out in full for you here:

"Then the kingdom of heaven shall be likened to ten virgins who took their lamps and went out to meet the bridegroom.

Now five of them were wise, and five were foolish.

Those who were foolish took their lamps and took no oil with them, but the wise took oil in their vessels with their lamps.

But while the bridegroom was delayed, they all slumbered and slept. "And at midnight a cry was heard: 'Behold, the bridegroom is coming; go out to meet him!'

Then all those virgins arose and trimmed their lamps. And the foolish said to the wise, 'Give us some of your oil, for our lamps are going out.' But the wise answered, saying, ' No, lest there should not be enough for us and you; but go rather to those who sell, and buy for yourselves.'

And while they went to buy, the bridegroom came, and those who were ready went in with him to the wedding; and the door was shut.

"Afterward the other virgins came also, saying, 'Lord, Lord, open to us!' But he answered and said, 'Assuredly, I say to you, I do not know you.'

"Watch therefore, for you know neither the day nor the hour in which the Son of Man is coming.

Matthew 25:1-13 NKJV

That is a chilling tale isn't it?

We can see in the parable again as we discussed in our first chapter the bridegroom saying to the foolish and unprepared virgins, *"I do not know you"*.

These foolish virgins are representative of many today who go along with the group and once may have stepped into God's Kingdom but for one reason or another haven't maintained a relationship with Jesus.

The oil that the virgins need for their lamps to work symbolises God's Spirit who we are one with.

Without a relationship with Jesus there is no Spirit in order to give life.

The parable is about being prepared at all times for The Lord's return - we need to be constantly filled and in relationship with Him.

We are told that no man knows exactly when Jesus will return.

How sad will we be if we are not ready and waiting for Him?

We can read about other virgins in connection with another wedding feast in the book of Solomon.

Let's find out.

Because of the fragrance of your good ointments, Your name is ointment poured forth; Therefore the virgins love you.

Song of Solomon 1:3 NKJV

The Song of Solomon is a beautiful love story about a bridegroom and His bride.

I really would encourage you to read the whole story.

Virgins represent the purity and holiness of the bride.

Purity and holiness accompanies the Bride as she prepares herself for the arrival of the Bridegroom.

It is because of the purity of the bride that the bridegroom is attractive to her.

In the story in the Song of Solomon purity is also referred to as a sweet smelling odour – it attracts the Bride to the Bridegroom and also the Bridegroom to the Bride.

We need to take note that it is the bride who prepares herself in order to be ready.

It is our own responsibility to adorn ourselves with purity and holiness.

We do that by being faithful to the Lord, by being obedient to Him, by spending time in His presence in order for His holiness to rub off on to us.

He is holy; therefore by constantly abiding in His presence, we too become holy.

Jesus said:

Blessed are the pure in heart.

God blesses those whose hearts are pure, for they will see God.

Matthew 5:8 NLT

In the book of Revelation we read:

Let us be glad and rejoice, and let us give honour to him. For the time has come for the wedding feast of the Lamb, and his bride has prepared herself.

She has been given the finest of pure white linen to wear." For the fine linen represents the good deeds of God's holy people.

And the angel said to me, "Write this:

Blessed are those who are invited to the wedding feast of the Lamb." And he added, "These are true words that come from God."

Revelation 19:7-9 NLT

The Wedding Feast

On another occasion Jesus was at a meal with many others and talked to them about a wedding feast to which many wealthy and noble people were invited.

In those days it was customary for a feast to be held before the wedding day.

The story is another illustration of God's Kingdom.

 I have copied the story in full for you:

Jesus said,

"God's kingdom is like a king who prepared a wedding feast for his son. He invited some people to the feast

When it was ready, the king sent his servants to tell the people to come. But they refused to come to the king's feast. "Then the king sent some more servants. He said to them, 'I have already invited the people.

So tell them that my feast is ready. I have killed my best bulls and calves to be eaten.

Everything is ready. Come to the wedding feast.'

"But when the servants told the people to come, they refused to listen. They all went to do other things.

One went to work in his field, and another went to his business.

Some of the other people grabbed the servants, beat them, and killed them.

The king was very angry. He sent his army to kill those who murdered his servants. And the army burned their city.

"After that the king said to his servants, 'The wedding feast is ready. I invited those people, but they were not good enough to come to my feast.

So go to the street corners and invite everyone you see. Tell them to come to my feast.'

So the servants went into the streets. They gathered all the people they could find, good and bad alike, and brought them to where the wedding feast was ready.

And the place was filled with guests.

"When the king came in to meet the guests, he saw a man there who was not dressed in the right clothes for a wedding. The king said, 'Friend, how were you allowed to come in here? You are not wearing the right clothes.'

But the man said nothing. So the king told some servants, 'Tie this man's hands and feet. Throw him out into the darkness, where people are crying and grinding their teeth with pain.'

Matthew 22:2-13 ERV

The same story can also be read in Luke ch. 14.

Jesus was feasting with Jewish people at the time and His story was by way of explaining to them how God had invited them to the feast but the Jewish nation had turned away from God and killed His prophets.

Jesus said in His story that "the meal was ready"!

All they had to do was to accept the invitation and turn up in order to enjoy it all. But they refused. They were too busy doing other things.

They crucified God's prophets and finally Jesus Himself.

Therefore God told His servants to invite anyone else that they could find; to invite the bad and the indifferent to come to the feast instead.

The feast was and is ready to eat. All that is required for the feast is guests.

The illustration is similar to the way that Jesus said on other occasions that "The Kingdom of God is at hand". "It is all prepared, ready to go"!

And so the servants went out and invited all and sundry to the feast instead.

This is exactly the good news that Jesus preached about and what has happened.

God has invited us to the wedding feast instead.

We are the ones who have been invited to the pre wedding feast.

The Jewish nation refused to accept Jesus. And yet the meal was ready.

It is ready to enjoy. It was ready when Jesus was on earth and it is still ready now.

Get your best clothes on people and come and eat!

The invitation is for all and sundry to come and eat at the wedding feast now.

You might be asking yourself, if the wedding feast is being enjoyed right now by many then when is the wedding?

It can't be too far away. Can it?

The wedding feast is all a part of the wedding ceremony itself.

Are we prepared and are we waiting for the bridegroom?

In the story that Jesus told there was one person at the wedding feast who was thrown out because he didn't have the correct clothes on.

There are some who simply go along with the crowd benefitting from the blessings that they are enjoying.

God looks into our hearts and knows those who are His.

He has provided the correct attire for us to wear at the feast - His Son's righteousness. If we aren't clothed in His righteousness and prefer to wear our own dirty rags then we won't be allowed to stay for long.

We might bluff our way through for a while but sooner or later we will be thrown out.

Paul referred to our 'good works' as being dirty rags.

What he meant was our own achievements – things that we do in our own strength or with our own abilities.

We need to clothe ourselves with Jesus.

After the wedding the Bridegroom and Bride will reign for one thousand years over all who remain on earth.

Great blessings belong to those who share in this first resurrection. They are God's holy people. The second death has no power over them. They will be priests for God and for Christ. They will rule with him for 1000 years.

Revelation 20:6 ERV

Eternity awaits.

How do we fit into this story?

A Summary

I once heard a preacher explain that the key to giving a good sermon came in four steps.

The first step was to explain what he was going to say.

He would then set out how he was going to say it.

Then he would say what he wanted to say.

After that he would explain what he had just said.

I'm not sure whether that was a good lesson or not but I will very briefly recall here a reminder of what we have discussed.

In all of the teaching and explanation within this book I have given scriptural references which I hope that you will look up, read and research yourself in order to confirm for yourselves that what you have read is correct.

I have also outlined the background of the events for you to give a better explanation.

I have purposefully not made reference to others research, teaching or authority as I am increasingly concerned that biblical teaching generally can very easily be both untrue and misunderstood.

Christian authors very often follow a generally understood historical guide which may or may not be correct. Indeed we have found in our own studies that many very basic belief systems and teaching within the established churches are profoundly incorrect.

We will be discussing these incorrect teachings within subsequent issues.

So let's just recap on what we have discovered so far:

1. We need to be aware of our place – Are we living within or outside of God's Kingdom?

2. Do we have or are we learning to have a relationship with Jesus?

3. Mankind rebelled against God and subsequently lost that unique relationship with Him.

4. Our own way of living stops us from having the relationship that we need and God wants with us.

5. God loves all of mankind and doesn't want to lose anyone therefore Jesus came in order to buy us back.

6. God's Kingdom is open for us now – today.

7. We are living in rebellion to God. In order to gain entry to God's Kingdom we need to realise that Jesus death paid for us.

8. God wants a relationship with us. The key to that relationship is learning to hear His voice and in being obedient.

9. When we enter His Kingdom through baptism we become truly one with Him – One with Spirit.

10. We are His disciples. We are also saints - Holy and set apart.

11. God has created the angels in order to be messengers and also to perform a host of other duties.

12. God has given us gifts – tools, in order to protect ourselves and to overcome the enemy who wants to destroy us.

13. We are born into God's Kingdom in order to have relationship with Him and with each other – we are His body – Jesus is the Head.

14. Relationship is the key to living in God's Kingdom not ritual or ceremony.

15. Jesus's death and resurrection overcame all of the enemy's work.

16. In partnership with God's Spirit we are now able to restore all things.

17. We are born into God's Kingdom in order to overcome the enemy and to throw down his strongholds.

18. God is Love. As we learn to be like Him we too take on His character which is love.

19. We are born into eternity.

20. What does eternity hold in store for us personally?

With each age has come a new move of God.

Many run with God's new revelation and enjoy His presence.

Then God moves on again but those involved with the previous blessing stay behind not noticing that Spirit has moved on.

This is how denominations are created – the church systems that are man's organisations.

God is continually moving forward.

If we are to live within His timing and His purpose then we also need to move forward with Him.

God is revealing a new thing to His people at this time of history.

God's Kingdom age is upon us.

It is time for each of us to take stock of where we stand in this period.

To be continued................

To contact Tim - the author - email: warwickhouse@mail.com

Tim has also written - **Journey into Life**

What did Jesus really preach about when He was on earth?

Within **A Journey into Life** we discover the joy of travelling to a new place.

Tim has set our search for Gods Kingdom in the form of a journey to a new land.

Once inside the new land we begin a journey of discovery – Everything is New.

Did Jesus teach that His Kingdom is within our grasp?

Is this a land – A Kingdom that we can live in now – in our own lifetime?

The answer is yes.

EBooks by Tim Sweetman

Journey into Life

Some adjustment required?

Other recommended publications of related interest:
By John J Sweetman
EBooks:
Establishing the Kingdom series:
  The Book of Joshua
  The Book of Judges
  The Book of Ruth
  The Book of 1 Samuel
  The Book of 2 Samuel
  The Book of 1 Corinthians
  The Book of 2 Corinthians
The Emerging Kingdom
Babylon or Jerusalem – your choice
Paperback books:
Babylon or Jerusalem – your choice
The Emerging Kingdom
Establishing the Kingdom series:
  The Book of Joshua
  The Book of Judges
  The Book of Ruth
  The Book of 1 Samuel
  The Book of 2 Samuel
  The Book of 1 Corinthians
  The Book of 2 Corinthians

by Fiona Sweetman – Paperback and EBook
  Taste the Colour Smell the Number

45390029R00094

Printed in Poland
by Amazon Fulfillment
Poland Sp. z o.o., Wrocław